LIMITLESS EXPECTATIONS

Discover How Your Beliefs Shape Your Reality and
Unlock the Power to Reprogram Your Mind for Success

KENT TODD CARPENTER

Copyright © 2024 by Kent Todd Carpenter

All rights reserved.

No portion of this book may be reproduced in any form without written permission from the publisher or author, except as permitted by U.S. copyright law.

DEDICATION

To my beautiful wife,
My quantum connection on this infinite journey. Mahal Kita

"Non est gravis scire omnium responsum—
est gravis scire reperire illum."
It is not important to know all the answers; what
matters is knowing how to find them.

QUANTUM CONNECTION

In the fabric of space, where time bends and sways,
Our souls are entangled in infinite ways.
A bond unseen, yet forever tight,
A dance of particles, both shadow and light.

No distance too vast, no silence too wide,
For you are the pulse in which I confide.
Through the chaos of stars, the void's gentle hum,
We are one equation, a singular sum.

This infinite journey, a path undefined,
We traverse together, both heart and mind.
Like waves on the shore, like light through the air,
You are my constant, my answer, my prayer.

Let the universe spin, its mysteries thrive,
In this connection, we endlessly thrive.
For love's the true quantum, no force can divide,
An infinite journey, with you by my side.

LIMITLESS EXPECTATIONS

THE MIRROR WITHIN

The world reflects what we hold inside,
A mirror of thoughts, where truths reside.
Beliefs we nurture, bright or grim,
Shape the path where dreams begin.
If we see walls, the road feels blocked,
But if we see doors, they will be unlocked.
A thought, a whisper, a seed unseen,
Grows to life where hope has been.
What we believe, we then create,
A force that bends the hands of fate.
Change the story, shift the view,
And watch the world align with you.

CONTENTS

INTRODUCTION   1

Limitless Expectations

Helping You Break Free from Limiting Beliefs

CHAPTER 1   5

Uncovering Your True Potential

Discover how to identify and break through self-imposed limitations.

CHAPTER 2   17

The Power of Belief - Rewriting Your Inner Script

Learn how your beliefs shape your reality and how to reprogram your mind for success.

CHAPTER 3   31

The Influence of Others - Building Emotional Resilience

Understand how others' opinions affect you and how to guard your inner peace.

CHAPTER 4   49

Setting Boundaries That Empower You

Master the art of setting healthy boundaries with people and situations that drain you.

CHAPTER 5   67

Embracing the Unknown: Fear as Fuel for Growth

How to use fear as a motivator to take bold, life-changing steps forward.

CHAPTER 6   83

Creating a Vision for Your Life

Step-by-step guidance on crafting a vision that excites and drives you.

CHAPTER 7   97

Mastering Your Mindset: From Fixed to Growth

How to shift from a limiting mindset to one of growth, possibility, and empowerment.

CHAPTER 8   107

Limitless Growth: How Challenges Shape Extraordinary Futures

Focusing on the boundless opportunities that emerge from overcoming struggles.

CHAPTER 9   117

The Art of Self-Compassion and Accountability

Cultivate a balanced approach of kindness and discipline to propel yourself forward.

CHAPTER 10   129

Living Authentically: Aligning Your Actions with Your Values

How to stay true to who you are while navigating a world full of external pressures.

CHAPTER 11   137

Limitless Living: Becoming the Best Version of Yourself

Embrace your journey of growth and transformation, applying all you've learned to create a fulfilling, purpose-driven life.

CHAPTER 12   147

The Role of Emotional and Spiritual Intelligence – Navigating Relationships and Challenges

Discover how Emotional Intelligence (EI) and Spiritual Intelligence (SI) shape personal and professional growth, enhancing resilience, relationships, and the ability to overcome life's challenges with purpose and empathy.

CHAPTER 13   169

The Energy of Gratitude: Transforming Your Outlook Through Appreciation

Understanding the power of gratitude in shifting your mindset and attracting opportunities.

CHAPTER 14   181

Limitless Horizons – Expanding Your Vision Beyond the Impossible

Conclude your journey by exploring the infinite possibilities that come with a limitless mindset.

CHAPTER 15   189

Embracing Infinity: Unlocking the Power of Limitless Expectations – Conclusion

A reflection on the parable of the boiling frog as a metaphor for the importance of awareness and taking decisive action in pursuit of a boundless future.

INTRODUCTION

Limitless Expectations

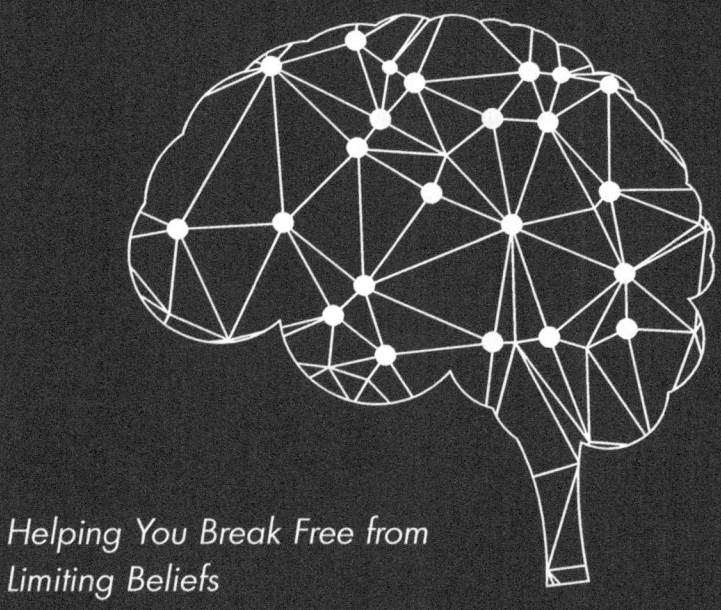

Helping You Break Free from Limiting Beliefs

Limiting beliefs are deeply rooted perceptions that define what we think we can or cannot achieve. These beliefs often originate from past experiences, societal expectations, or internalized criticism. Overcoming them requires self-awareness, emotional honesty, and the courage to replace them with empowering perspectives.

The journey begins with a willingness to take action. Without the willingness to take action, your efforts become meaningless—like trying to take a shower while wearing a raincoat. Start small and consistently challenge the beliefs that hold you back. If you fear failure, try something new and embrace the lessons it brings. Remember the acronym F.E.A.R.—False Evidence Appearing Real. This phrase emphasizes that fear often arises from imagined or exaggerated perceptions rather than reality. By recognizing this, you can reframe fear as an opportunity to question limiting beliefs and overcome them.

With determination and the right mindset, you can overcome limiting beliefs and unlock your true potential. To achieve this, it's essential to connect with your authentic self and embrace personal growth. Begin by engaging in self-reflection to identify your strengths, passions, and values. Practices like journaling or meditation can help you gain clarity and deepen your understanding of who you are.

Adopt a mindset that views challenges as opportunities rather than obstacles. Keeping a positive outlook will allow you to find joy and gratitude in the process of overcoming difficulties. Shift your perspective—replace *"I have to do this" with "I get to do this."* This simple reframing transforms tasks into privileges, fostering motivation and enthusiasm.

Your beliefs are the lens through which you perceive the world, and they play a powerful role in shaping your reality. What you believe about yourself, others, and the possibilities in life directly influences your thoughts, decisions, and actions. When you hold empowering beliefs, you are more likely to take risks, embrace opportunities, and persevere through challenges. Conversely, limiting beliefs can create barriers, keeping you stuck in cycles of doubt and inaction. Reprogramming your mind for success begins with identifying these limiting beliefs and challenging their validity.

Replace them with positive, constructive beliefs that align with your goals and values. Visualization, affirmations, and consistent action can help reinforce this new mindset, gradually rewiring your brain to support your growth and success. By transforming your belief system, you open the door to new possibilities and create a reality aligned with your highest potential.

This quote highlights the importance of releasing attachments to false identities and beliefs in order to grow into our potential.

On Letting Go of False Beliefs:
"When I let go of what I am, I become what I might be."
— *Tao Te Ching by Lao Tzu: (Chapter 44)*

CHAPTER 1

Uncovering Your True Potential

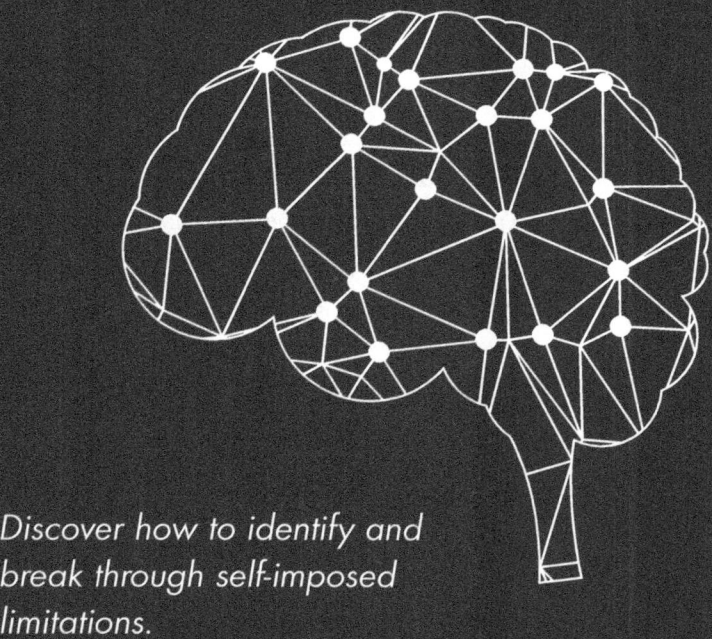

Discover how to identify and break through self-imposed limitations.

Recognizing Your Limiting Beliefs

Limiting beliefs are like invisible walls—barriers that keep you from stepping into your full potential. They are the persistent thoughts and assumptions we hold about ourselves and the world, often learned in childhood or shaped by past experiences. These beliefs can be incredibly powerful, dictating the choices we make, the risks we take, and the limits we place on ourselves. In this chapter, we will explore what limiting beliefs are, how to identify them, and the steps you can take to break free of their constraints. We'll also draw inspiration from some real-life examples of famous people and even insects, showing how overcoming limiting beliefs can lead to extraordinary results.

What Are Limiting Beliefs?

Limiting beliefs are those convictions or assumptions that restrict your ability to reach your goals. These beliefs can be overt, like "I'm not good enough," "I'll never succeed," or "I don't deserve happiness." Or, they can be subtle, like assuming you're not the type of person who takes risks or believing you don't have the right skills to pursue a particular career.

These beliefs shape the way we see ourselves and our potential. For example, someone who believes "I'll never be good enough" might avoid pursuing a new job, taking on a challenging project, or even learning a new skill because they've already convinced themselves it's not possible. The interesting thing about limiting beliefs is that they often operate on autopilot—they become so ingrained that we don't even question them. Over time, they dictate our behavior, turning into self-fulfilling prophecies.

How to Identify Limiting Beliefs

Recognizing limiting beliefs is the first step in breaking free from them. To identify them, you must pay close attention to your thoughts and language, especially when you face challenges or try something new.

One key indicator is negative self-talk. When you attempt to step outside your comfort zone—whether it's applying for a new job, starting a new project, or pursuing a dream—you might catch yourself saying things like:

- "I'll never be successful."
- "I don't have what it takes."
- "It's too risky."
- "I'm not smart enough to do this."

These thoughts are signs of limiting beliefs at play. Often, limiting beliefs are the excuses we make to avoid stepping outside our comfort zone. They are often rooted in fear—fear of failure, fear of judgment, or fear of not being good enough.

One powerful way to uncover limiting beliefs is by paying attention to patterns in your life. Do you consistently avoid certain opportunities because of fear or doubt? Do you tend to procrastinate on projects or goals that could move your life forward? This can be a sign that an underlying belief is keeping you stuck.

For example, one of the most famous cases of overcoming limiting beliefs comes from the world of sports. **Michael Jordan**, widely considered the greatest basketball player of all time, was cut from his high school basketball team. At the time, it was easy for him to accept that he wasn't good enough, and many people probably assumed he wouldn't make it. But instead of allowing this to limit him, Jordan used the setback as motivation to work harder. He pushed through his self-doubt, and his persistence led him to become a legend in the NBA.

Action Step: Write Down Your Limiting Beliefs

One of the most effective ways to confront limiting beliefs is to get them out of your head and onto paper. This will give you clarity and the opportunity to examine them from a fresh perspective. Here's a simple exercise:

1. Write down the beliefs that consistently hold you back.

These might include thoughts like "I'm not worthy," "I'll never be successful," or "It's too late for me." Be specific about the thoughts or phrases that arise when you consider going after your dreams or pursuing new goals.

2. Ask yourself, "Is this belief true?"

Challenge the validity of the belief. For example, if you think, "I'm not good enough to start my own business," ask yourself, "Is this belief true? Have I seen anyone who has started a business from scratch and succeeded?"

A great example of this challenge comes from **Mr. Beast, born Jimmy Donaldson**, he overcame numerous challenges to become one of the most successful content creators on YouTube. Starting with little recognition, he spent years studying the platform's algorithm and experimenting with content before finding his breakthrough. Despite facing financial struggles early on, he reinvested his earnings into creating increasingly ambitious and philanthropic projects, showcasing his determination and creativity. His battle with Crohn's disease has also shaped his perspective, teaching him resilience and the importance of maintaining balance in life. Today, Mr. Beast inspires millions by proving that persistence, innovation, and generosity can lead to extraordinary success.

Find examples that contradict the belief.

Look for real-life evidence that disproves your limiting belief. For instance, if you believe you can't achieve success in a creative field because you lack the right talent, research others who started without formal training but went on to become successful.

Consider the story of **J.K. Rowling**, the author of the ***Harry Potter*** series. Before becoming one of the world's most famous authors, Rowling faced numerous rejections and doubted her own ability to succeed. She even struggled with feelings of inadequacy as a single mother. Yet, she continued to write and believe in her story, ultimately changing the landscape of literature.

Inspiration from the Natural World

Sometimes, nature offers powerful examples of overcoming limits that are worth considering. Let's take the example of insects—creatures with seemingly small, limited potential—yet they demonstrate some of the most resilient behaviors in the animal kingdom.

The **bombardier beetle** is a perfect example. When threatened, it releases a chemical spray from its abdomen at a temperature of nearly 100°C (212°F), making it one of the few creatures able to defend itself against much larger predators. Despite its small size and perceived fragility, the beetle overcomes its limits by using an ingenious survival mechanism.

Likewise, the **migrating monarch butterfly** doesn't allow its diminutive size or frailty to hold it back. Monarchs travel thousands of miles across North America to reach their wintering grounds in Mexico. The journey, often fraught with danger, is an incredible feat of perseverance and strength, reminding us that size and past experiences don't necessarily define our potential.

Both of these insects exemplify the idea that overcoming our limitations is often a matter of utilizing inner resources and taking bold steps in the face of adversity. They don't sit back and accept their boundaries—they find ways to push past them.

A Cautionary Tale of Limiting Beliefs in Human History

Limiting beliefs have repeatedly shaped human history, often obstructing progress and innovation. Yet, time and again, such thinking has been challenged and ultimately overcome, leading to transformative breakthroughs. These historical examples stand as powerful reminders of humanity's resilience—the ability to confront challenges, dispel limiting beliefs, and embrace new ways of thinking and being.

1. Copernicus and the Geocentric Model

Limiting Belief: For centuries, the geocentric model—believing Earth was the center of the universe—dominated scientific thought, largely supported by Ptolemaic astronomy and reinforced by religious authorities.

Impact: This belief limited humanity's understanding of the cosmos, holding back scientific advancements in astronomy and physics.

Breakthrough: Nicolaus Copernicus challenged this notion with his heliocentric theory, which placed the Sun at the center of the solar system. His work laid the foundation for future astronomers like Galileo and Kepler, who provided further evidence for this paradigm shift.

2. Louis Pasteur and Germ Theory vs. Humoral Medicine

Limiting Belief: Ancient Greek practices of balancing bodily fluids (humors) and treatments like bloodletting dominated Western medicine for centuries. The belief that disease was caused by an imbalance of humors (blood, phlegm, yellow bile, black bile) hindered the development of effective medical treatments.

Impact: These misconceptions led to harmful practices like bloodletting and prevented the adoption of more scientific approaches to disease. On December 14, 1799, President George Washington passed away at his home following a brief illness and extensive blood loss—about 40 percent of his blood—due to bloodletting.

Breakthrough: Louis Pasteur's germ theory of disease demonstrated that microorganisms, not imbalances in bodily fluids, caused illness. This discovery revolutionized medicine, leading to advancements in hygiene, vaccination, and antibiotic treatments.

3. Spontaneous Generation of Life (e.g., Mice from Corn)

Limiting Belief: For centuries, people believed in spontaneous generation—the idea that living organisms could arise from non-living matter. For example, it was thought that mice could evolve from sacks of corn or that maggots spontaneously appeared in rotting meat.

Impact: This belief hindered the study of biology by promoting pseudoscientific explanations for life's origins.

Breakthrough: Francesco Redi and later Louis Pasteur debunked spontaneous generation. Redi's experiments in the 17th century showed that maggots came from fly eggs, not spontaneously from meat. Pasteur's work conclusively disproved spontaneous generation, establishing the principle of biogenesis (life comes from life).

4. The Impossibility of Flight

Limiting Belief: For centuries, it was believed that human flight was impossible. Many scientists and engineers thought heavier-than-air machines could never overcome gravity.

Impact: This belief delayed innovations in aviation and limited humanity's vision for the skies.

Breakthrough: The Wright brothers proved the skeptics wrong in 1903 by achieving controlled, sustained, powered flight. Their success ushered in the modern era of aviation.

These examples demonstrate how **challenging** deeply held but false beliefs, has been a crucial driver of progress throughout history. **Overcoming limiting ideas** requires curiosity, evidence, and the courage to think differently. Recognizing and questioning limiting beliefs opens the door to new understanding and personal growth.

> **On False Beliefs and New Ideas** (*Confucius*):
> "Real knowledge is to know the extent of one's ignorance."

Recognizing Your Limiting Beliefs

Identifying and breaking through self-imposed limitations is a crucial step in unlocking your true potential. Here's a practical approach to how you can do this:

1. Recognize Your Limiting Beliefs

- **What They Are**: Limiting beliefs are deeply ingrained convictions or assumptions that prevent you from pursuing goals or taking risks. These might sound like, "I'm not good enough," "I'll never succeed," or "I don't deserve happiness."
- **How to Identify Them:** Pay attention to your thoughts and language, especially when you face challenges or try something new. If you catch yourself saying or thinking things that sound like excuses or self-doubt, that's often a sign of a limiting belief at play.
- **Action Step:** *Write down the beliefs that consistently hold you back. Ask yourself, "Is this belief true?" Challenge its validity by finding examples that contradict it.*

2. Shift Your Perspective

- **What It Means:** Changing how you see yourself, your capabilities, and the world around you is essential to breaking through limitations. Instead of seeing challenges as roadblocks, see them as opportunities for growth.
- **How to Shift:** Reframe negative thoughts into positive, empowering ones. For example, instead of thinking "I can't do this," try "This is difficult, but I can learn and grow from it."
- **Action Step:** *When you encounter a challenge, ask yourself: "What can I learn from this? How can this help me grow?" Practice focusing on progress, not perfection.*

3. Expand Your Comfort Zone Gradually

- **What It Means:** Growth happens outside your comfort zone, but stepping into unfamiliar territory can feel scary. The key is to take small, incremental steps to stretch beyond your usual limits.
- **How to Expand:** Set small, achievable goals that push your boundaries. As you accomplish them, your confidence will build, and you'll begin to realize that your perceived limitations were often self-imposed.
- **Action Step:** *If public speaking terrifies you, start by speaking in front of a mirror, then to a friend, and eventually to a small group. With each step, you'll feel more comfortable.*

4. Address Fear Head-On

- **What It Means**: Fear is one of the primary forces behind self-imposed limitations. It holds you back from trying new things or pursuing your goals. Acknowledge that fear is natural but shouldn't control your actions.
- **How to Confront It:** Examine the fear: Is it based on fact or assumption? Often, fear is rooted in irrational thinking. By facing it directly and breaking it down, you'll see that many fears are not as powerful as they seem.
- **Action Step:** *Practice taking one brave action every day, even if it's small. Each step reduces the grip of fear and builds your courage.*

5. Cultivate a Growth Mindset

- **What It Means:** A growth mindset is the belief that abilities and intelligence can be developed with effort and perseverance. People with this mindset embrace challenges, learn from feedback, and persist through setbacks.
- **How to Cultivate It:** Focus on the process of learning and growing rather than on immediate success or failure. See mistakes as opportunities for improvement, not as evidence of inadequacy.

- **Action Step:** *When you encounter setbacks, remind yourself that they are part of the learning journey. Use the mantra: "I am capable of learning and improving."*

6. Surround Yourself with Supportive People

- **What It Means:** The people you surround yourself with can either reinforce your self-imposed limitations or encourage you to break through them. Positive, supportive people push you to be your best, while toxic relationships can perpetuate self-doubt.
- **How to Build Support:** Seek out mentors, friends, or communities that uplift you, challenge you, and help you grow. Distance yourself from those who reinforce negativity.
- **Action Step:** *Join groups or networks that align with your goals, and actively seek mentorship from individuals who have overcome similar challenges.*

7. Set Bold, Yet Achievable Goals

- **What It Means:** Setting goals is essential for breaking through limitations. But setting goals that are too small or too large can undermine your efforts. Aim for goals that are just beyond your current abilities to encourage growth, but still achievable.
- **How to Set Goals**: Break your larger vision into smaller, manageable steps. Focus on the process rather than the outcome to keep your motivation high.
- **Action Step:** *Set one short-term goal that pushes you beyond your comfort zone and take the first step towards it today.*

8. Practice Self-Compassion

- **What It Means**: Being kind to yourself is key to overcoming limitations. If you're too hard on yourself when you make mistakes, it reinforces the belief that you're not capable of succeeding.

- **How to Practice It:** Treat yourself with the same kindness and understanding that you would offer a friend. Recognize that setbacks and imperfections are part of growth.
- **Action Step:** *When you fail or face setbacks, say to yourself, "This is part of the process. I'll learn and try again."*

9. Visualize Your Success

- **What It Means:** Visualization helps you break through limitations by mentally rehearsing success and creating a clear image of what's possible. It prepares your mind to take action toward your goals.
- **How to Visualize:** Close your eyes and vividly imagine yourself achieving your goals. Feel the emotions associated with your success. This mental practice can make it feel more attainable and motivate you to act.
- **Action Step**: *Spend 5-10 minutes daily visualizing your success, seeing yourself overcoming obstacles and reaching your goals.*

10. Commit to Continuous Growth

- **What It Means:** True personal growth is a lifelong journey. By consistently pushing past your limits, you develop the resilience and self-belief to unlock your potential.
- **How to Commit:** Embrace learning and self-improvement as a constant part of your life. Never stop seeking ways to challenge yourself and grow.
- **Action Step:** *Dedicate time each week to learning something new, whether it's through reading, courses, or experiences that stretch your capabilities.*

"Your assumptions are your windows on the world. Scrub them off every once in a while, or the light won't come in."
– Isaac Asimov

Conclusion: Break Free and Live Boldly

Limiting beliefs are powerful, but they don't define you. By recognizing them, challenging their validity, and replacing them with more empowering thoughts, you can transform your approach to life. Just like Michael Jordan, J.K. Rowling, and the bombardier beetle, you have the potential to defy the limits you've placed on yourself.

Remember: limiting beliefs are often rooted in fear, but courage grows when you take action. You are capable of achieving far more than you may believe. The first step is to recognize your limiting beliefs—and then move forward with the knowledge that you can overcome them.

This quote serves as a reminder that often the barriers we face are not external, but self-imposed. It's a call to challenge and transcend our own limiting beliefs.

"The only limits that exist are the ones you place on yourself."
—Unknown

CHAPTER 2

The Power of Belief - Rewriting Your Inner Script

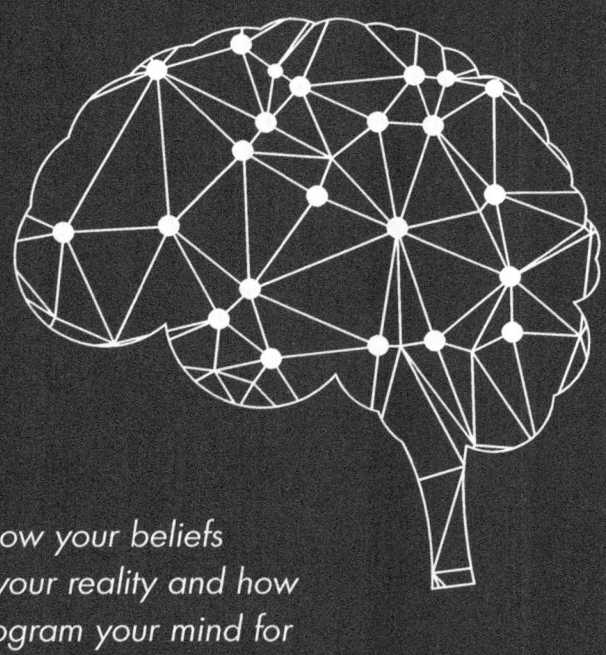

Learn how your beliefs shape your reality and how to reprogram your mind for success.

A person's beliefs are among the most powerful forces shaping their reality. They act as filters through which we interpret the world, influencing the way we think, behave, and react to experiences. In essence, beliefs form the lens through which we view everything—from our potential for success to how we navigate challenges. When we hold empowering beliefs, such as self-confidence, optimism, or a growth mindset, they encourage us to take risks, persist through setbacks, and approach life with curiosity and creativity. These beliefs can propel us to achieve great things, as they shape our thoughts and actions in ways that align with our goals. For example, a person who believes they can learn and grow is more likely to embrace challenges, view failures as opportunities for learning, and ultimately succeed in areas they once thought impossible.

On the other hand, limiting beliefs—such as fear of failure, low self-worth, or doubt—can create significant obstacles in our lives. These beliefs can cause us to shy away from opportunities, avoid taking risks, and even sabotage our own progress. For instance, someone who believes they are not smart enough to succeed in a challenging career might hesitate to pursue that path altogether, without ever giving themselves the chance to succeed. Our beliefs about ourselves, our abilities, and the world around us directly shape our actions and, ultimately, our reality. This dynamic is evident throughout history, with figures like **Plato** and **Socrates** exemplifying the power of belief in shaping their intellectual pursuits and, by extension, the world. Socrates, for instance, held the belief that the unexamined life was not worth living, a conviction that led him to question the very foundations of knowledge, ethics, and society, ultimately shaping Western philosophy.

Reprogramming the mind for success and rewriting one's inner script involves shifting these deeply held beliefs toward ones that serve growth, resilience, and achievement. A powerful first step is recognizing and challenging limiting beliefs. Just as Plato believed in the importance of self-awareness and reason, individuals today can gain insight into their beliefs through self-reflection and mindfulness. By becoming aware of negative thought patterns, we can begin to replace them with more empowering alternatives. Affirmations and visualization are potent tools in this process. By consciously affirming our strengths, goals, and potential, and by visualizing our success, we begin to rewire our subconscious minds to align with our aspirations.

In nature, this concept is mirrored in the transformation of a caterpillar into a butterfly. The caterpillar's belief, if it had one, might be rooted in its physical form and limitations, but through a process of metamorphosis, it transcends its current state, emerging as something entirely different, capable of flying. In the same way, humans, too, have the capacity to transcend limiting beliefs and transform their inner narratives. History is full of examples of individuals who redefined their beliefs and, in doing so, changed the course of their lives and the world. **Walt Disney**, for instance, faced repeated setbacks and rejection before building his entertainment empire. Early in his career, he was fired from a newspaper job for **"lacking creativity,"** and his first animation company went bankrupt. Despite these failures, Disney held an unshakable belief in his vision of creating a magical world of storytelling and innovation. His determination to bring his dreams to life, paired with his resilience and creativity, led to the creation of one of the most influential entertainment companies in history. Disney's journey demonstrates how belief and perseverance can turn dreams into reality, even in the face of repeated adversity.

By actively cultivating positive beliefs, whether through affirmations, taking bold actions, or surrounding ourselves with supportive influences, we can reshape our inner script. The process is not instantaneous, but over time, as we embrace new, empowering beliefs, we begin to see our potential and reality shift toward greater success and fulfillment. Just as the greatest philosophers, inventors, and leaders in history transformed their belief systems to shape their futures, so too can each individual tap into the transformative power of belief to create a life aligned with their true potential.

To program the mind for success and rewrite one's inner script, a few strategies can be employed:

1. Awareness

Begin by identifying and understanding the beliefs that are currently shaping your reality. Are they serving your goals? Self-reflection and mindfulness can help uncover limiting patterns.

Awareness is the key to breaking free from automatic, negative thought patterns and creating space for new, positive beliefs that foster growth, resilience, and success. To program the mind for success and rewrite one's inner script, the first essential step is cultivating awareness. This involves taking the time to reflect on and identify the beliefs that currently shape your thoughts and actions. Beliefs are often deeply ingrained and may go unnoticed until we consciously examine them. Self-reflection and mindfulness are powerful tools for this process. By observing our inner dialogue, paying attention to recurring thoughts, and noticing how we respond to various situations, we can begin to uncover the limiting beliefs that hold us back. These may include thoughts like "I'll only be happy when I achieve_____" or "I'm too damaged or broken to heal," which quietly shape our actions and prevent us from pursuing opportunities. Recognizing these limiting patterns is the first step in dismantling them and replacing them with more empowering beliefs.

Once we are aware of the beliefs influencing our behavior, we can assess whether they are truly serving our goals. Do they align with the person we want to become or the success we hope to achieve? If they don't, it's time to challenge and transform them. The process requires consistent effort, but as we consciously shift our mindset, we begin to create a reality that supports our aspirations. By replacing limiting beliefs with empowering ones, we set the foundation for personal transformation and unlock our potential to succeed.

2. Challenge Limiting Beliefs

Question the validity of negative or limiting beliefs. Often, they are based on past experiences, societal influences, or fears rather than objective truths. Replacing them with empowering beliefs involves recognizing their roots and choosing new, more supportive perspectives.

Challenging limiting beliefs is a crucial step in rewiring the mind for success. Many of the beliefs that hold us back are rooted in past experiences, societal conditioning, or irrational fears, rather than in objective truths. For example, a person may hold a belief that they are not capable of achieving success in a particular field because of a past failure or because society has told them it's too difficult. These beliefs can become so ingrained that they feel like absolute truths, even though they may not reflect reality. The first step in challenging these beliefs is to recognize where they originated—whether from childhood, past experiences, or external pressures—and understand that they may not be universally true or relevant to our current situation. By questioning the validity of these beliefs, we can begin to dismantle their power over our actions and mindset.

Once we've identified and questioned the roots of limiting beliefs, the next step is to replace them with empowering, supportive beliefs. This requires consciously choosing to adopt new perspectives that align with our goals and potential. For instance, if the limiting belief is "I'm not good enough," it can be replaced with a more empowering belief like "I am capable of learning and growing through challenges." Replacing old beliefs is not a one-time event but an ongoing process of self-reinforcement. Through affirmations, positive self-talk, and aligning our actions with our new beliefs, we gradually reshape our inner narrative. This shift in mindset can unlock new possibilities, allowing us to take risks, seize opportunities, and move forward with confidence. By consistently challenging and replacing limiting beliefs, we create a foundation for lasting personal transformation and success.

3. Affirmations and Visualization

Positive affirmations and visualization techniques can help rewire the subconscious mind. Repeating affirmations that reflect desired outcomes can reinforce new beliefs, while visualizing success helps create a mental image of the future you want to manifest.

Affirmations and visualization are powerful tools for transforming the subconscious mind and shaping a positive future. Repeating affirmations—statements that reflect your desired outcomes—can help replace limiting beliefs with empowering ones. For example, saying, "I am capable of achieving my goals" consistently can instill confidence and resilience. Visualization takes this process a step further by allowing you to mentally rehearse your success. When you vividly imagine the details of your goals—whether it's landing a dream job, excelling in a sport, or building meaningful relationships—you send a clear signal to your brain, aligning your thoughts and actions with your aspirations. Together, affirmations and visualization serve as a foundation for creating a mindset primed for success.

A remarkable example of visualization in action is Walt Disney, who famously envisioned a world of magic and creativity long before it materialized. Despite facing numerous setbacks, including financial struggles and failed ventures.

Disney's vivid imagination and ability to visualize his dream of Disneyland kept him endlessly motivated. In his mind's eye, he could clearly see Cinderella's Castle standing proudly, hear the laughter of children enjoying the Jungle Cruise, and even picture the lush jungle springing to life. He could feel the joy and wonder his creations would bring to people all around the world, fueling his determination to turn his vision into reality.

This clarity of vision guided his decisions and helped him overcome challenges, such as skepticism from investors and competitors. His unwavering belief in his vision turned what seemed impossible into a reality that continues to inspire millions. Affirmations and visualization are not just for dreamers but also for anyone seeking to make meaningful changes in their lives.

For instance, an athlete preparing for a competition might visualize themselves crossing the finish line, hearing the roar of the crowd, and feeling the exhilaration of victory. Coupled with affirmations like "I am strong and capable," this practice reinforces their mental strength and focus. Similarly, an entrepreneur launching a new business can visualize a thriving enterprise, successful meetings, and satisfied customers, paired with affirmations such as "I am creating value and achieving success." These techniques help rewire the subconscious mind, foster determination, and guide actions toward turning aspirations into achievements.

4. Positive Self-Talk

Replacing negative self-talk with constructive, encouraging dialogue strengthens a belief system that supports success. Focus on empowering language that emphasizes growth, learning, and achievement.

Positive self-talk is a transformative practice that replaces negativity with empowering and constructive internal dialogue. By shifting focus from self-doubt to self-belief, positive self-talk strengthens the mental foundation necessary for achieving success. It involves recognizing negative thoughts and consciously reframing them into affirmations that emphasize growth, learning, and resilience. For instance, instead of saying, "I can't do this," one might say, "I am learning and growing stronger every day." This shift in mindset not only enhances confidence but also reduces stress, making it easier to stay focused and motivated, even in challenging situations.

Athletes are prime examples of individuals who harness the power of positive self-talk to overcome setbacks and achieve success. **Golf legend Tiger Woods** is known for his mental resilience and use of positive self-talk to maintain focus during high-pressure moments. In interviews, Woods has often highlighted how he replaces doubts with affirmations such as "I trust my training" or "I've done this before." This mental discipline has helped him win numerous championships, even when faced with physical injuries or intense competition. Similarly, tennis champion **Serena Williams** uses positive self-talk to boost her confidence, frequently reminding herself to stay strong and focused during matches. Her ability to encourage herself through internal dialogue has played a crucial role in her record-breaking career.

The impact of positive self-talk extends beyond athletics and can be applied to anyone striving for personal or professional growth. For example, an amateur golfer working to improve their game might remind themselves, "Every shot is a chance to learn," rather than dwelling on missed opportunities. This mindset fosters perseverance and a growth-oriented attitude. Likewise, a student preparing for a challenging exam could replace self-defeating thoughts like "I'm not smart enough" with "I am prepared, and I will give my best effort." By focusing on constructive and encouraging language, individuals can cultivate a belief system that supports success and helps them navigate challenges with resilience and determination.

5. Surround Yourself with Positivity

The people, environments, and media you expose yourself to all influence your belief systems. Surrounding yourself with supportive, positive influences can help reinforce new beliefs and behaviors.

The "inputs" we receive—through the media we consume, the environments we inhabit, and the thoughts we entertain—profoundly shape our beliefs, attitudes, and behaviors. If we expose ourselves to negativity, harmful influences, or limiting beliefs, the "output" of our thoughts and actions will likely reflect that negativity. Conversely, surrounding ourselves with positive influences, constructive ideas, and empowering beliefs can lead to growth, creativity, and success.

For example, consuming uplifting books, engaging with supportive communities, and practicing positive affirmations are ways to ensure that the "input" into the mind fosters healthy, productive "output." As with computers, the quality of what we put into our minds directly affects what we get out of them. This analogy underscores the importance of mindfulness in choosing what we expose ourselves to, reinforcing the age-old adage: *"You are what you think."*

Surrounding yourself with positivity is a transformative practice that significantly shapes your mindset and belief systems. The people you interact with, the environments you inhabit, and the media you consume all have the power to influence your thoughts and actions. By choosing supportive friends, uplifting spaces, and inspiring content, you create a foundation that nurtures growth and success. Positive influences encourage you to believe in yourself, overcome challenges, and stay focused on your goals. This deliberate choice to seek out positivity is a catalyst for cultivating resilience and fostering an optimistic outlook on life.

Taylor Swift exemplifies the power of surrounding oneself with positivity. Known not just for her incredible music career but also for her generosity and kindness, Swift actively creates an uplifting environment around her. Recently, she gave $100,000 bonuses to her concert staff, acknowledging their hard work and dedication during her record-breaking Eras Tour. This act of generosity reflects her commitment to building a supportive and appreciative community. Moreover, Swift's consistent charity work, from donating millions to disaster relief efforts to supporting education, demonstrates how she uses her success to spread positivity. By surrounding herself with like-minded individuals who share her values and passion for making a difference, she reinforces a belief system rooted in gratitude, kindness, and empowerment.

Taylor Swift's career success also highlights how surrounding oneself with positivity can lead to accomplishing ambitious goals. Despite facing public scrutiny and professional setbacks, Swift has built a network of supportive collaborators and fans who uplift and inspire her. She focuses on creating music that resonates with audiences while staying true to her values. Her decision to re-record her albums to reclaim her artistic ownership is a testament to her determination and resilience. Through her actions and the environment, she cultivates, Swift proves that surrounding yourself with positivity is not just a strategy for personal happiness but also a cornerstone for achieving lasting success.

6. Take Consistent Action

Beliefs are reinforced through experience. By taking consistent action aligned with your new beliefs, you validate and strengthen them. Success comes from incremental steps, persistence, and learning from setbacks.

Taking consistent action is essential for reinforcing and solidifying new beliefs. When you align your actions with your aspirations and values, you create experiences that validate and strengthen those beliefs. Each step you take, no matter how small, contributes to building confidence and momentum. This process requires persistence and a willingness to embrace setbacks as opportunities for learning and growth. Over time, these consistent efforts compound, leading to tangible progress and a deep sense of accomplishment.

History is filled with examples of individuals who took consistent action aligned with their new beliefs, ultimately achieving extraordinary success. **Mahatma Gandhi**, for instance, believed in nonviolent resistance as a powerful tool for social and political change. Despite facing immense opposition and personal sacrifice, Gandhi consistently acted in accordance with his belief in peaceful protest. His commitment to this principle not only reinforced his own resolve but also inspired millions to join him in India's struggle for independence. Gandhi's success demonstrates how persistence and alignment between belief and action can lead to transformative change. A quote often attributed to Mahatma Gandhi is:

> **"Be the change you wish to see in the world."**

While this phrasing is widely associated with Gandhi, it is actually a paraphrase of his teachings rather than a direct quote. The closest documented statement by Gandhi is:

> **"If we could change ourselves, the tendencies in the world would also change. As a man changes his own nature, so does the attitude of the world change towards him. This is the divine mystery supreme. A**

wonderful thing it is and the source of our happiness. We need not wait to see what others do."

This reflects the same spirit of personal responsibility and transformative action. It's a powerful reminder that meaningful change begins within ourselves.

Another example is Thomas Edison, whose belief in innovation and determination led to the invention of the practical electric light bulb. Edison famously remarked, "I have not failed. I've just found 10,000 ways that won't work." This mindset exemplifies the power of taking consistent action despite setbacks. Every experiment, whether successful or not, reinforced Edison's belief in his ability to solve the problem. Through persistence and incremental progress, he achieved breakthroughs that revolutionized modern life. These examples from history highlight how taking action aligned with one's beliefs is not only a validation of those beliefs but also a pathway to meaningful and lasting success.

7. Mindfulness and Meditation

Practicing mindfulness helps increase self-awareness and offers a deeper understanding of the mind's habitual patterns. Meditation can also promote a calm, focused state that allows for better emotional regulation and conscious thought restructuring.

Mindfulness and meditation are transformative practices that foster a profound connection between the mind and present moment awareness. Mindfulness involves focusing your attention on the present, observing thoughts, feelings, and sensations without judgment. It cultivates self-awareness, helping you recognize habitual patterns of thought and behavior. This awareness creates a space for conscious choice, allowing you to respond to situations with clarity rather than reacting impulsively. For example, recognizing the onset of stress during a busy day and pausing to take a few deep breaths can prevent feelings of overwhelm, enabling a more composed and productive approach.

Meditation, a practice that often complements mindfulness, deepens this sense of self-awareness and inner calm. By focusing on a specific anchor, such as the breath or a mantra, meditation trains the mind to gently redirect itself when distracted. Over time, this practice enhances emotional regulation and improves cognitive focus. Research has shown that meditation can lower levels of stress hormones, reduce symptoms of anxiety and depression, and even improve physical health by decreasing blood pressure and inflammation. For instance, someone struggling with anxiety might find relief through regular meditation, as it helps them observe anxious thoughts without being consumed by them, fostering a sense of control and peace.

The positive effects of mindfulness and meditation extend to all aspects of life, enhancing well-being and enriching relationships. Mindful practices encourage a nonjudgmental attitude, promoting compassion toward oneself and others. This can improve communication and reduce conflicts in personal and professional settings. Additionally, meditation fosters resilience by helping individuals navigate challenges with a balanced perspective. Athletes, for example, use mindfulness to stay present during high-pressure moments, and professionals rely on meditation to maintain focus and creativity amidst demanding schedules. These practices empower individuals to live intentionally, fostering a harmonious state of mind and a healthier, more fulfilling life.

By actively reshaping beliefs and thought patterns, it's possible to shift the inner narrative and develop a mindset that fosters success. The process of rewriting one's inner script takes time and consistent effort, but with persistence, it leads to lasting change and greater alignment with personal goals.

Conclusion:
The Transformative Power of Belief: Aligning Mindset, Action, and Positivity for Success

Beliefs are powerful forces shaping our reality, acting as filters that influence thoughts, actions, and responses to experiences. Empowering beliefs, such as self-confidence and a growth mindset, inspire action, resilience, and curiosity, fostering success. In contrast, limiting beliefs, rooted in fear or doubt, can hinder progress and prevent opportunities. Rewriting one's inner script involves becoming aware of and challenging these limiting beliefs, replacing them with affirming and supportive alternatives. Techniques like mindfulness, affirmations, and visualization help reshape these thought patterns, enabling individuals to align their subconscious with their goals and aspirations.

Historical and contemporary examples illustrate the transformative power of belief and consistent action. Figures like Mahatma Gandhi and Thomas Edison achieved extraordinary success by aligning their actions with empowering beliefs and persisting despite setbacks. Gandhi's commitment to nonviolence and Edison's belief in innovation demonstrate how taking incremental, purposeful steps reinforces belief systems and leads to transformative outcomes. Similarly, modern examples like Taylor Swift emphasize the importance of surrounding oneself with positivity, creating environments and relationships that nurture growth, resilience, and success.

Practices like mindfulness and meditation further enhance this process by fostering self-awareness and emotional regulation. Mindfulness helps individuals recognize habitual thought patterns, while meditation promotes focus and calm, enabling better responses to challenges. Together, these tools empower individuals to cultivate resilience, reframe their inner narratives, and achieve fulfillment. By consistently reshaping beliefs, taking aligned actions, and fostering positive influences, it is possible to create a life of growth, success, and well-being.

A central teaching from Hindu philosophy, this directly illustrates the profound impact beliefs have on shaping identity and destiny.

"Man is made by his belief. As he believes, so he is."
– Bhagavad Gita

CHAPTER 3

The Influence of Others - Building Emotional Resilience

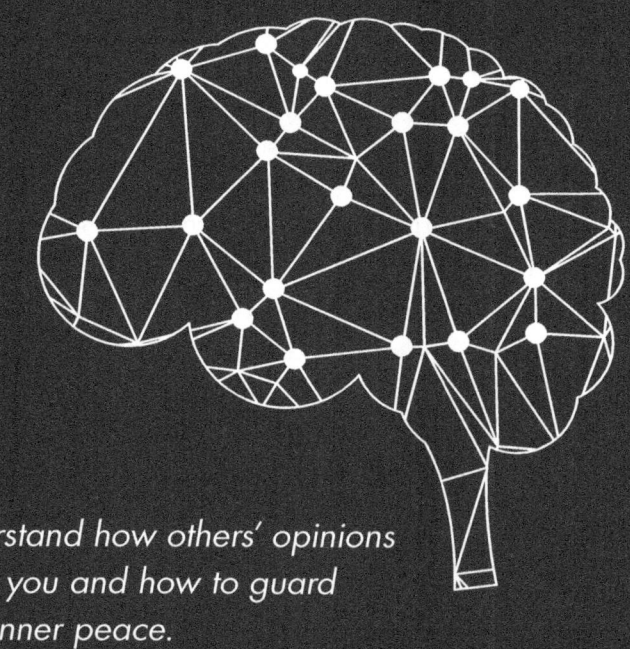

Understand how others' opinions affect you and how to guard your inner peace.

How the Opinions of Others Can Impact Emotional Resilience

The opinions of others can significantly influence a person's self-perception, confidence, and emotional well-being. While feedback and perspectives can be helpful, excessive sensitivity to others' opinions can undermine emotional resilience. Here's how:

Eroding Self-Worth

Constant criticism or negative opinions can lead to self-doubt, making individuals question their abilities and worth. Over time, this can chip away at confidence and create a fear of failure or rejection. Eroding self-worth through constant criticism or negative opinions can have profound and lasting effects on a person's confidence and emotional well-being. When individuals are frequently subjected to harsh judgments, they may begin to internalize those opinions, questioning their abilities and worth. Over time, this can lead to a persistent fear of failure or rejection, making them hesitant to take risks or assert themselves. This erosion of self-worth often leaves individuals feeling stuck, unable to pursue opportunities or trust their instincts, as they have become overly reliant on external validation.

A well-known example of this can be seen in the life of Kurt Warner's rise to NFL stardom is a story of resilience and unwavering self-belief in the face of repeated rejection. Before becoming a two-time NFL MVP and a Super Bowl champion, Warner faced numerous setbacks that could have easily eroded his self-worth. After going undrafted in the 1994 NFL Draft, he was cut from the Green Bay Packers during training camp and struggled to find opportunities in professional football. To make ends meet, Warner worked as a grocery store stock clerk, earning $5.50 an hour, while holding onto the hope of playing football professionally.

Criticism from coaches and scouts who doubted his ability to succeed at the professional level compounded his challenges. Many believed he lacked the skills and athleticism needed to compete in the NFL. Despite these doubts, Warner refused to let others define his worth. He continued to hone his skills in the Arena Football League and later the NFL Europe League, using every opportunity to improve and prove himself. His persistence paid off when he signed with the St. Louis Rams, eventually leading them to a Super Bowl victory in 1999. Warner's improbable journey earned him a reputation as one of the greatest underdog stories in sports history.

Kurt Warner's story illustrates how resilience and self-belief can shield someone from the damaging effects of external criticism. By focusing on his work ethic and trusting in his abilities, Warner overcame the doubts of others to achieve extraordinary success. His journey serves as a reminder that self-worth is not determined by outside opinions but by one's own dedication and perseverance. Warner's path from stocking shelves to the NFL Hall of Fame stands as a testament to the power of inner strength in the face of adversity.

Dependency on External Validation

When people overly rely on the approval of others, their emotional stability becomes tied to external factors. This dependency makes them more vulnerable to fluctuations in praise or criticism.

Dependency on external validation can significantly impact emotional well-being, as it ties self-worth and stability to the opinions and judgments of others. When someone relies heavily on external approval, their sense of value becomes contingent on factors outside their control. While positive feedback may provide temporary boosts in confidence, the absence of praise—or the presence of criticism—can lead to anxiety, self-doubt, and emotional instability. This cycle creates a fragile foundation for self-esteem, making individuals susceptible to fluctuations in their mood and self-image based on how others perceive them.

A well-documented example of this phenomenon is seen in the concept of ***contingent self-esteem* in psychology**. Research has shown that individuals whose self-worth is highly contingent on external validation, such as academic performance or physical appearance, often experience heightened stress and depressive symptoms when they encounter failure or negative feedback. A classic study on college students found that those who sought validation through high grades felt elated with success but deeply discouraged when they received lower marks. Their emotional well-being depended not on their intrinsic efforts or learning but on the approval symbolized by external recognition.

This principle is also illustrated in the life of Princess Diana. As a young royal, Diana initially struggled with her sense of identity, as her self-worth was often shaped by public opinion and media attention. Her emotional health fluctuated with the intense scrutiny and praise she received as a global icon. Over time, Diana worked to cultivate a stronger sense of self by focusing on her values, such as her humanitarian work and role as a mother, rather than relying solely on external validation. Her journey highlights the importance of building an internal sense of worth, independent of external factors, to maintain emotional resilience and stability.

By focusing on intrinsic motivations and aligning actions with personal values, individuals can break free from the dependency on external validation. Developing self-awareness, practicing self-compassion, and surrounding oneself with supportive relationships can help create a foundation of self-worth that is steady and reliable, regardless of external opinions.

Nature offers profound examples of resilience and self-sufficiency that can illustrate the pitfalls of dependency on external validation and the power of intrinsic stability.

1. The Bamboo Tree: Strength from Within

The bamboo tree provides a powerful metaphor for intrinsic strength. In its first years, bamboo spends most of its energy growing deep roots underground, unseen by the outside world. During this time, there's no visible growth above the surface, which might be misjudged as a lack of progress. However, once its roots are fully established, bamboo can grow several feet in just weeks. This mirrors the importance of cultivating a strong foundation within ourselves rather than relying on the validation of visible progress or external praise. Bamboo's reliance on its internal root system demonstrates the power of focusing on intrinsic growth over external validation.

2. The Sunflower: Turning Toward Inner Growth

Sunflowers are famous for their heliotropism—they turn toward the sun as it moves across the sky. But during cloudy days, when the sun isn't visible, sunflowers don't stop growing. Instead, they align themselves with one another, sharing resources and sustaining growth through their own systems. This ability to thrive despite external conditions reminds us that even when external validation (the "sun") is absent, we can rely on our internal resources and supportive environments to sustain us. It shows the importance of building resilience and finding strength from within, even when external sources of encouragement are unavailable.

3. The Salmon: Persevering Without Approval

Salmon, during their spawning journey, face tremendous challenges such as strong currents, predators, and natural obstacles. Their drive to swim upstream doesn't come from any external reward or approval but from an internal instinct and purpose. Salmon push forward despite adversity, focusing solely on their intrinsic goal of reaching their spawning grounds to continue the life cycle. This perseverance exemplifies the importance of staying true to one's purpose, regardless of external conditions or obstacles.

Heightened Anxiety and Stress

Worrying about what others think can lead to anxiety, as individuals may constantly second-guess their choices and suppress their authentic selves to conform to others' expectations.

Worrying excessively about others' opinions can create heightened anxiety and stress, as individuals feel a constant need to second-guess their decisions to meet perceived expectations. This fear of judgment often results in suppressing one's authentic self, leading to a state of internal conflict. When people focus more on pleasing others than on their own values or desires, they lose a sense of autonomy, which is essential for emotional well-being. Over time, this can create a cycle of stress and dissatisfaction, as the need for external approval becomes insatiable.

A real-life example of this phenomenon can be seen in the psychological concept of **social anxiety disorder**, where individuals experience intense fear of being judged, embarrassed, or humiliated in social situations. One study found that people with high levels of social anxiety often conform to others' expectations, even if it conflicts with their personal beliefs or desires, to avoid criticism. For example, a student may avoid asking questions in class for fear of appearing unintelligent, despite knowing that seeking clarity would benefit their understanding. This self-suppression not only limits personal growth but also exacerbates feelings of inadequacy, perpetuating the anxiety. To mitigate this cycle, it is crucial to develop self-awareness and practice authenticity.

Building confidence in one's own choices, irrespective of external judgment, can significantly reduce stress. Techniques such as mindfulness and **cognitive behavioral therapy** (CBT) are effective in addressing anxiety related to external opinions. For instance, CBT helps individuals reframe negative thoughts and challenge the validity of their fears, fostering a healthier relationship with their own self-perception. By focusing on personal values rather than societal expectations, individuals can regain their sense of autonomy, reducing anxiety and creating space for genuine self-expression.

Adele: Turning Anxiety into Art

Adele, one of the most celebrated singers of her generation, has openly shared her struggles with severe stage fright and social anxiety, revealing a deeply human side to her towering success. Despite her immense talent and numerous accolades, Adele has described feeling physically ill and experiencing panic attacks before live performances. Her anxiety was particularly intense in the early years of her career when she faced the daunting pressure of performing in front of large crowds. In interviews, she has admitted to shaking, crying, and even questioning her ability to take the stage moments before her shows.

Rather than allowing her anxiety to define her, Adele found ways to channel her nerves into her music. She uses her performances as an outlet for her emotions, transforming vulnerability into a powerful connection with her audience. Adele's authenticity and relatability have resonated with millions of fans worldwide. Songs like *Someone Like You* and *Hello* not only showcase her vocal prowess but also reveal the raw emotion that has become her signature. This connection helps her push through her anxiety, as she focuses on the joy her music brings to others rather than her own fears.

While Adele acknowledges that she still experiences anxiety, she has embraced it as part of who she is. Instead of trying to eliminate her fears, she works to manage them, often engaging in rituals or breathing exercises before performances to center herself. Her journey reminds us that success is not the absence of fear but the courage to move forward despite it. By being open about her struggles, Adele has not only inspired fans but also broken-down stigmas around anxiety, proving that even the most successful individuals face challenges and can thrive by embracing their vulnerabilities. Her story is a testament to the power of passion, perseverance, and authenticity.

Donny Osmond: From Anxiety to Confidence

Donny Osmond, a household name as a member of the Osmond family, faced intense pressure from an early age as he grew up in the constant spotlight of fame. Known for his boyish charm and immense talent, Donny was thrust into stardom during his teenage years, performing on stage and television alongside his siblings. However, the demands of his career and the expectation to maintain a flawless public persona began to take a toll on his mental health. Donny developed social anxiety, frequently worrying about how he was perceived by fans, critics, and even his family. This anxiety often led him to question his worth beyond his carefully crafted public image.

The turning point came when Donny recognized the need to prioritize his mental well-being. He sought help through therapy, where he learned to address the root causes of his anxiety and reframe his relationship with external validation. He also adopted mindfulness practices, which helped him stay grounded and focus on the present moment. By shifting his perspective from pleasing others to finding his own happiness and fulfillment, Donny gradually regained his confidence. This internal work allowed him to reconnect with his love for performing on his terms, without being consumed by the fear of judgment.

With his renewed sense of self, Donny went on to achieve incredible success in his solo career, including chart-topping hits and a long-running Las Vegas residency with his sister, Marie Osmond. Their show became a testament to his ability to thrive under the same spotlight that once fueled his anxiety. By sharing his journey openly, Donny has inspired others to seek help and embrace authenticity, proving that it's possible to overcome even deep-seated fears to achieve lasting success and joy. His story is a powerful reminder of the importance of self-awareness, resilience, and prioritizing one's inner peace over external pressures.

Stifling Growth

Overemphasis on others' opinions can discourage risk-taking and experimentation. Fear of judgment may prevent individuals from pursuing goals or expressing their creativity, leading to stagnation.

Overvaluing the opinions of others can become a substantial obstacle to personal growth, as it often inhibits risk-taking and stifles experimentation. When individuals are overly concerned about how they might be judged, they often hesitate to step outside their comfort zones or try new things. This fear of failure or ridicule fosters a mindset focused on avoiding mistakes rather than embracing opportunities for learning and development. Over time, this apprehension can lead to stagnation, as individuals miss chances to expand their skills, pursue their goals, or unlock their full potential.

An environment overly focused on external validation can also stifle creativity, a vital component of personal and professional growth. When people tailor their ideas and actions to fit societal norms or others' expectations, they risk suppressing their unique perspectives and innovations.

This fear of standing out or being criticized often leads to conformity, limiting the diversity of thought and creativity needed for breakthroughs. For instance, someone with a passion for entrepreneurship may abandon their business idea out of fear that it might fail or be ridiculed, never realizing its potential success.

One striking example of overcoming this dynamic comes from Vincent van Gogh. During his lifetime, van Gogh faced harsh criticism and indifference toward his art, which prevented him from achieving success. Despite this lack of validation, he continued to experiment and pursue his vision, creating groundbreaking work that was only appreciated after his death. His story underscores the importance of focusing on one's intrinsic motivations rather than external opinions. By letting go of the fear of judgment, individuals can take bold steps toward their goals, express their creativity fully, and experience the profound growth that comes from embracing both successes and failures.

Guarding Your Inner Peace

Maintaining inner peace in the face of external opinions requires intentional practices that cultivate self-awareness, confidence, and emotional boundaries. Here's how:

Strengthen Self-Awareness

Understand your values, goals, and priorities. When you have a clear sense of who you are, it's easier to filter out opinions that don't align with your true self.

The Foundation of Inner Clarity

Self-awareness is the cornerstone of personal growth and emotional resilience. It involves understanding your values, goals, and priorities, which serve as a compass for navigating life's challenges and decisions. When you have a clear sense of who you are, it becomes much easier to filter out external opinions or expectations that don't align with your authentic self. Without self-awareness, individuals are often swayed by external influences, losing touch with their inner voice and risking decisions that may lead to dissatisfaction or regret.

In psychology, self-awareness is deeply tied to emotional intelligence, which is the ability to recognize and regulate one's emotions while understanding the emotions of others. Daniel Goleman, a psychologist and emotional intelligence expert, emphasizes that self-awareness is the foundation of this skill. For example, an emotionally intelligent leader may reflect on their priorities and realize they value collaboration over competition, helping them lead with integrity and authenticity. By understanding what drives them, such individuals can focus their energy on choices that resonate with their core values, regardless of external pressures.

One compelling example of self-awareness in action is the concept of ***self-concordance*** from goal-setting theory. Research shows that people who pursue goals aligned with their intrinsic values experience greater satisfaction and motivation compared to those who pursue externally motivated goals, such as seeking approval or avoiding judgment. For instance, a student who chooses a field of study based on personal passion, rather than societal expectations, is more likely to remain engaged and persist through challenges. By prioritizing their own values, they filter out external pressures and align their actions with their true self.

To strengthen self-awareness, reflective practices like journaling, mindfulness, and seeking feedback from trusted individuals are invaluable tools. For example, journaling can help individuals clarify their thoughts and recognize patterns in their behavior. Mindfulness, on the other hand, encourages nonjudgmental observation of one's feelings and reactions, fostering deeper understanding. Together, these practices help individuals identify their authentic goals and values, allowing them to make decisions rooted in clarity and purpose. By cultivating self-awareness, people gain the confidence to stay true to themselves and navigate life with a stronger sense of direction.

Practice Emotional Boundaries

Learn to distinguish between constructive feedback and unwarranted criticism. Not every opinion deserves your attention or emotional investment.

Protecting Your Inner Peace

Emotional boundaries are essential for maintaining mental and emotional well-being, especially in a world where unsolicited opinions are common. Not every opinion deserves your attention or emotional investment, as many come from a place of bias, misunderstanding, or personal projection. Learning to distinguish between constructive feedback, which can help you grow, and unwarranted criticism, which serves no real purpose, is a skill that empowers you to stay grounded and focused on your goals. By establishing boundaries, you safeguard your sense of self and prevent the energy drain that comes from engaging with every piece of feedback.

History offers countless examples of individuals who faced unsolicited opinions and criticism, yet managed to rise above them by practicing emotional boundaries. One famous case is **Marie Curie**, the first woman to win a Nobel Prize and the only person to win in two scientific fields (Physics and Chemistry). Despite her groundbreaking discoveries in radioactivity, Curie faced harsh criticism not only for her work but also for her personal life. Many dismissed her contributions simply because she was a woman in a male-dominated field. Furthermore, after her husband's death, her personal relationships were scrutinized by the press, overshadowing her scientific achievements. By focusing on her passion for science and refusing to let unwarranted criticism derail her, Curie continued her pioneering research and left an indelible mark on the world.

Another example is **Abraham Lincoln**, who faced relentless criticism during his presidency. From being ridiculed for his appearance and background to being doubted for his decisions during the Civil War, Lincoln endured a barrage of unsolicited opinions. He famously said, *"I do the very best I know how—the very best I can; and I mean to keep doing so until the end."* This mindset reflects his ability to practice emotional boundaries, focusing on constructive feedback while ignoring baseless critiques. By maintaining his composure and staying committed to his vision, Lincoln preserved the Union and abolished slavery, achieving monumental success despite the noise of his detractors.

These historical figures teach us the value of discernment when it comes to opinions. Constructive feedback can offer valuable insights, but unwarranted criticism often reflects the critic's insecurities rather than your own shortcomings. By recognizing this, you can conserve your emotional energy and focus on what truly matters—your goals, values, and growth. Practicing emotional boundaries is not about ignoring all feedback but about being selective with what you internalize, ensuring you remain resilient and purposeful in the face of external judgment.

Cultivate Self-Compassion

Treat yourself with kindness and forgiveness. When you accept your imperfections, others' opinions lose their power to diminish your self-worth.

Self-compassion is the practice of treating yourself with kindness, understanding, and forgiveness, especially during moments of failure or doubt. It involves recognizing that imperfection is a universal human experience and that mistakes are opportunities for growth, not reflections of your worth. When you develop self-compassion, you build an inner sanctuary of acceptance that shields you from the harmful effects of external criticism. By being your own source of support, you can maintain emotional resilience and a strong sense of self-worth, regardless of others' opinions.

One of the key benefits of self-compassion is that it diminishes the power of external judgments. When you accept yourself fully, flaws and all, you no longer need validation from others to feel worthy. For example, a professional facing negative feedback at work might initially feel discouraged, but self-compassion allows them to reframe the experience as a chance to learn rather than a personal failure. Instead of internalizing the criticism, they can focus on their strengths and take constructive action. This mindset not only preserves their self-esteem but also encourages growth and improvement.

History and psychology both provide examples of the transformative power of self-compassion. The psychologist **Kristin Neff**, a leading researcher on self-compassion, found that people who practice self-kindness are better equipped to handle setbacks and are less likely to experience anxiety or depression.

By cultivating self-compassion, you create a foundation of emotional stability that isn't swayed by the opinions of others. Treating yourself with kindness allows you to embrace your imperfections and acknowledge your intrinsic worth. This inner strength not only fosters personal growth but also empowers you to approach challenges and criticisms with grace and confidence. In a world often quick to judge, self-compassion serves as a powerful tool for maintaining your peace, authenticity, and resilience.

Focus on Your Inner Circle

Surround yourself with supportive and uplifting individuals whose opinions are rooted in care and encouragement. A strong support system can reinforce resilience.

Building a Foundation of Support

The people you surround yourself with have a profound impact on your emotional well-being and resilience. When your inner circle consists of supportive and uplifting individuals, their encouragement provides a buffer against the negativity and challenges of the outside world. Unlike superficial acquaintances or critical voices, these trusted individuals offer constructive feedback rooted in genuine care. Their belief in your abilities and goals can help you stay grounded, build confidence, and navigate difficult times with greater ease.

A strong support system acts as an anchor, reinforcing your resilience during moments of self-doubt or adversity. For example, consider the story of **Helen Keller**, who became a symbol of perseverance despite being blind and deaf from an early age. Her teacher and lifelong companion, Anne Sullivan, was a key member of her inner circle, offering unwavering encouragement and guidance. Sullivan's support helped Keller overcome immense obstacles, allowing her to achieve remarkable success as an author, speaker, and activist. This relationship illustrates how the presence of even one supportive person can profoundly shape someone's ability to persevere and thrive.

By focusing on your inner circle, you can prioritize relationships that nurture positivity and growth while distancing yourself from toxic influences. Surrounding yourself with people who genuinely care about your success creates an environment where resilience can flourish. These relationships remind you of your strengths, offer constructive guidance when needed, and provide a safe space to express yourself authentically. A supportive inner circle is more than a network of allies; it is a source of inspiration and motivation, reinforcing your ability to overcome challenges and pursue your goals with confidence.

Limit External Noise:

Reduce exposure to sources of negativity, whether it's critical social media, toxic environments, or individuals who drain your energy. Curating your environment can help protect your peace.

Protecting Your Peace in a Digital Age

In today's hyperconnected world, we're constantly bombarded with opinions, criticism, and negativity, especially through social media. For teenagers in particular, the digital world can amplify feelings of inadequacy, exclusion, and self-doubt, making it a significant contributor to emotional distress. Studies have shown a troubling connection between social media overexposure and rising rates of anxiety, depression, and even suicide among teens. Platforms designed for connection often become breeding grounds for cyberbullying, unhealthy comparisons, and external validation. Reducing exposure to this noise by setting boundaries around social media use is critical for protecting emotional well-being.

One key aspect of limiting external noise involves recognizing and addressing "emotional vampires"—individuals who drain your energy through constant negativity, criticism, or excessive demands. These people may not intend harm, but their behavior can leave you feeling emotionally depleted and overwhelmed. For example, a coworker who constantly complains or a friend who thrives on drama can pull you into their negativity, leaving little room for your emotional well-being. Setting boundaries with such individuals is crucial. This might involve limiting interactions, changing the subject when conversations turn toxic, or even reevaluating the relationship if it consistently affects your peace of mind.

Reducing external noise also means curating the media you consume and the environments you frequent. Social media, while a great tool for connection, is often a breeding ground for comparison, judgment, and negativity. Unfollowing accounts that make you feel inadequate or trigger anxiety can be a simple but transformative step. Similarly, avoiding toxic environments, whether in personal or professional settings, can help you focus on what truly matters. By intentionally surrounding yourself with uplifting people, content, and spaces, you prioritize your mental health and create a foundation for emotional stability. Limiting external noise allows you to reclaim your energy, stay aligned with your goals, and thrive in a world filled with distractions.

Develop Mindfulness Practices:

Techniques such as meditation, deep breathing, or journaling can help you center yourself and detach from external opinions. These practices foster a stronger connection to your inner world.

Reconnecting with Your Inner Self

Mindfulness is the practice of bringing your attention to the present moment, free from judgment or distraction. It serves as a powerful antidote to the chaos of external opinions and the pressures of modern life. Techniques such as meditation, deep breathing, and journaling allow you to center yourself and foster a deeper connection with your inner world. When you practice mindfulness, you gain the ability to observe your thoughts and emotions without being controlled by them. This detachment helps you focus on your values and aspirations rather than being swayed by external noise or fleeting judgments.

The Tao Te Ching offers profound wisdom on the importance of mindfulness and inner peace. **Lao Tzu** writes, *"At the center of your being, you have the answer; you know who you are, and you know what you want."* This teaching reminds us that true clarity and direction come not from external validation but from looking within. Mindfulness practices like meditation allow us to access this center of being, where self-awareness and authenticity reside. By regularly engaging in these practices, you cultivate a calm, focused state that enhances emotional resilience and helps you navigate challenges with grace.

The Bhagavad Gita also emphasizes the importance of mindfulness and detachment. In one of its most famous teachings, Krishna advises Arjuna to act without attachment to the results of his actions: *"You have the right to perform your duty, but not to the fruits of your actions."* This principle encourages focusing on the present moment and performing your best without being consumed by others' opinions or expectations. Journaling, for example, can be a practical way to reflect on your actions, clarify your intentions, and let go of external outcomes. By cultivating mindfulness through these practices, you strengthen your inner foundation, enabling you to live with purpose and peace regardless of external circumstances.

Celebrate Your Authenticity:

Embrace your unique qualities and understand that not everyone will agree with your choices—and that's okay. Authenticity is more fulfilling than universal approval.

The Power of Being True to Yourself

Embracing your authenticity means recognizing and valuing your unique qualities, passions, and beliefs, even in the face of disagreement or judgment. In a world that often pressures individuals to conform, authenticity can feel like a bold and courageous choice. However, staying true to yourself is far more fulfilling than chasing universal approval, which is often fleeting and conditional. By celebrating your individuality, you align your actions with your values, fostering a sense of inner peace and purpose that external validation cannot replicate.

History offers us a remarkable example of authenticity in **Nikola Tesla**, a brilliant inventor who stayed true to his vision despite widespread skepticism and criticism. Tesla was often considered eccentric due to his unorthodox methods, ambitious ideas, and introverted nature. While contemporaries like Thomas Edison sought fame and fortune, Tesla focused on advancing humanity through his groundbreaking work with alternating current (AC) electricity, wireless communication, and renewable energy. His vision of a world powered by free, limitless energy was revolutionary, but it clashed with the profit-driven motives of his time, leading to significant opposition and financial struggles. Despite public ridicule and isolation, Tesla refused to compromise his values or conform to societal expectations, leaving behind a legacy of innovation that shaped modern technology.

Tesla's story underscores the importance of embracing your authenticity, even when it comes at a cost. While he did not achieve widespread recognition during his lifetime, his commitment to his principles and passion for discovery ultimately earned him posthumous admiration as one of history's greatest inventors. His life reminds us that authenticity often involves taking the less-traveled road, one that might not win immediate approval but leads to a deeper sense of fulfillment and long-term impact. By celebrating your authenticity, you honor your true self and inspire others to do the same, proving that staying true to your unique path is always worth it.

Conclusion

By cultivating self-awareness, setting emotional boundaries, and nurturing inner strength, individuals can protect their inner peace and build lasting resilience against external judgments. Self-awareness allows you to align your thoughts and actions with your values, serving as a compass that keeps you grounded amid differing opinions. Emotional boundaries help you filter constructive feedback from unwarranted criticism, preventing the energy drain that comes from trying to please everyone. When you prioritize your own values and aspirations over fleeting external judgments, you create a foundation of authenticity and self-confidence. This inner clarity enables you to navigate challenges with grace, remaining true to yourself regardless of the noise around you.

This quote emphasizes the importance of inner strength and self-awareness, reminding us that our resilience and identity are shaped not by external opinions, but by our own values and inner fortitude. It's a powerful reminder to focus on cultivating your inner world, even in the face of external challenges.

"What lies behind us and what lies before us are tiny matters compared to what lies within us."
– Ralph Waldo Emerson

CHAPTER 4

Setting Boundaries That Empower You

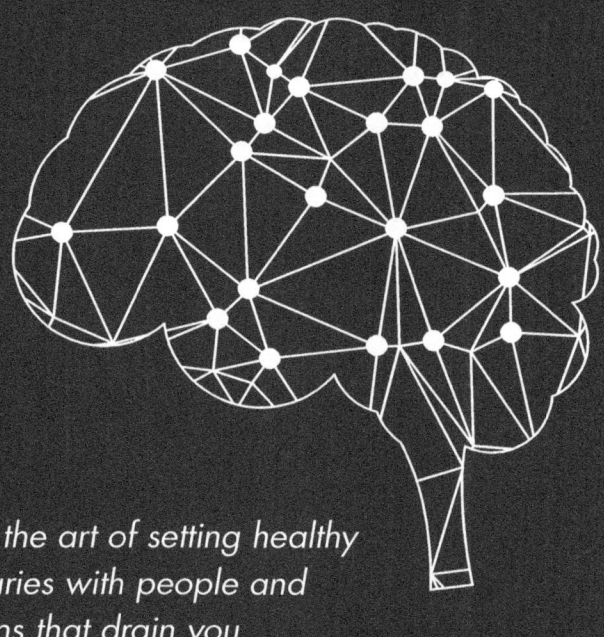

Master the art of setting healthy boundaries with people and situations that drain you.

Setting healthy boundaries is crucial for maintaining emotional well-being, safeguarding your energy, and nurturing positive relationships in all areas of life. Boundaries act as guidelines that define what is acceptable and unacceptable in interactions, helping you prioritize your needs and values. They empower you to communicate your limits clearly and assertively, ensuring that others respect your space and time. By establishing boundaries, you create a balance between giving and receiving, preventing burnout and resentment. Whether in personal relationships, at work, or in social settings, healthy boundaries foster mutual respect, reduce stress, and provide a framework for authentic connections. Ultimately, boundaries are an act of self-care that enable you to protect your inner peace while engaging meaningfully with the world around you.

Here's how a person can establish and maintain empowering boundaries with family, co-workers, bosses, and draining individuals or situations:

1. Understanding Your Needs and Limits: The Foundation of Healthy Boundaries

Self-awareness is the cornerstone of understanding your needs and limits, empowering you to navigate relationships and environments with clarity and confidence. By reflecting on your values, priorities, and emotional triggers, you can identify what energizes you versus what drains you. This process of introspection allows you to pinpoint areas in your life where boundaries are needed to protect your emotional well-being. For example, if constant interruptions at work leave you feeling frustrated or unproductive, recognizing this trigger helps you set limits to safeguard your focus. Psychology supports this idea, as self-awareness is a key component of emotional intelligence, which enables individuals to regulate their emotions and make decisions aligned with their values.

Once you've identified your needs, the next step is to clarify your limits. This involves being specific about what behaviors or situations you find acceptable or unacceptable in various contexts, such as work, family, or friendships. For instance, at work, you might decide that you're comfortable sharing project updates but prefer to keep personal matters private. Similarly, in your personal life, you may set a limit on how much time or emotional energy you can invest in family obligations without compromising your self-care. The psychological concept of *assertiveness* is essential here, as it helps individuals express their limits clearly and confidently, without aggression or passivity.

Understanding and articulating your needs and limits is not only about protecting yourself but also about fostering healthier relationships. When you communicate your boundaries, you create a framework for mutual respect and understanding. This reduces the likelihood of misunderstandings and resentment, while promoting a sense of empowerment. Cognitive-behavioral therapy (CBT) techniques often encourage individuals to practice boundary-setting as a way to combat stress and improve emotional resilience. By knowing and respecting your own limits, you create a balanced life that honors both your personal well-being and your relationships.

Key Takeaways: Understanding Your Needs and Limits

- **Self-Awareness:** Begin by reflecting on your values, priorities, and emotional triggers. Understanding what drains you versus what energizes you helps clarify where boundaries are needed.
- **Clarify Your Limits:** Be specific about what behaviors or situations you find acceptable or unacceptable. For instance, decide how much personal information you're comfortable sharing at work or how much time you're willing to spend on family obligations.

2. Communicate Clearly and Assertively: Building Healthy Interactions

Effective communication is essential for setting and maintaining boundaries in relationships. Clear and assertive communication allows you to express your needs directly while fostering mutual respect. Using "I" statements is a powerful technique in this process, as it focuses on your feelings and needs rather than blaming others. For example, saying, *"I need uninterrupted time to focus on this task,"* conveys your requirement without putting the other person on the defensive. This aligns with principles in psychology, particularly nonviolent communication (NVC), which emphasizes expressing needs with clarity and empathy to resolve conflicts constructively.

Specificity is equally important when setting boundaries, as ambiguity can lead to misunderstandings and unmet expectations. For instance, telling a colleague, *"I'm happy to help, but I need 24 hours' notice for additional tasks,"* is far more effective than saying, *"I'll see what I can do."* By being specific, you provide clear guidelines, reducing the likelihood of confusion or frustration on both sides. This approach is reinforced in assertiveness training, a psychological technique that teaches individuals to articulate their needs clearly while respecting others' perspectives. It empowers individuals to create healthy, balanced relationships without sacrificing their well-being.

A real-life example of clear and assertive communication comes from the workplace dynamics of **Sheryl Sandberg, former COO of Meta (Facebook).** Sandberg is known for advocating open communication and boundary-setting as part of effective leadership. In her book Lean In, she shares how she learned to set boundaries with her time by saying, "I need to leave at 5:30 PM to have dinner with my kids," rather than offering vague excuses. This directness not only ensured her personal priorities were met but also set an example for others to respect their own boundaries. Her calm, respectful, and specific communication style demonstrates how assertiveness can lead to better understanding and collaboration in both professional and personal relationships.

Clear and assertive communication is not just about stating your needs—it's about doing so in a way that builds trust and respect. By using "I" statements, being specific, and maintaining composure, you create an environment where your boundaries are understood and honored. This approach fosters healthier relationships and enhances emotional resilience, enabling you to navigate conflicts and interactions with confidence and clarity.

Key Takeaways: Communicate Clearly and Assertively

- **Use "I" Statements:** Express your needs in a way that is direct but respectful. For example, instead of saying, "You always interrupt me," say, "I need uninterrupted time to focus on this task."
- **Be Specific:** Ambiguity can lead to misunderstandings. For instance, tell a co-worker, "I'm happy to help, but I need 24 hours' notice for additional tasks," rather than a vague, "I'll try."
- **Stay Calm:** Emotions can run high when setting boundaries, especially with family or authority figures. Maintain a calm and composed tone to ensure your message is heard clearly.

3. Learn to Say No Without Guilt: The Power of Assertiveness

Learning to say no is an essential skill for maintaining emotional well-being and personal boundaries. Often, people feel obligated to agree to every request, fearing they might disappoint others or be seen as selfish. However, saying no is not an act of selfishness but one of self-care. It allows you to prioritize your needs, energy, and goals, ensuring that your commitments align with your values. Polite refusals, such as "I can't commit to that right now" or "I'd love to help, but I need to focus on my current priorities," convey respect while affirming your boundaries. This approach reinforces self-respect and builds healthier relationships rooted in mutual understanding.

From a psychological perspective, the inability to say no often stems from people-pleasing tendencies, rooted in fear of rejection or conflict. Assertiveness training, a common technique in cognitive-behavioral therapy (CBT), helps individuals develop the confidence to express their needs and preferences clearly. Being assertive doesn't mean being aggressive; it's about balancing your rights with the rights of others. By practicing polite but firm refusals, you reduce the likelihood of overextending yourself and experiencing burnout. Over time, this skill not only strengthens your emotional resilience but also fosters respect from others, as they come to understand and honor your boundaries.

A real-life example of learning to say no comes from Coach **Mike Ditka**, a legendary figure in the NFL, offers a compelling example of learning to say no and prioritizing his personal and professional values. During his tenure as head coach of the Chicago Bears, Ditka was known for his fiery personality and relentless commitment to excellence. However, as his fame grew, he faced increasing demands on his time—from media appearances and endorsement deals to speaking engagements. Early in his career, Ditka often felt compelled to say yes to these opportunities, viewing them as part of the job and a way to expand his influence. However, this nonstop schedule began to interfere with his ability to focus on coaching and maintain balance in his personal life.

Ditka eventually realized the importance of setting boundaries and saying no to commitments that didn't align with his core priorities—his team, his family, and his health. He became more selective about where he directed his energy, focusing on activities that truly mattered to him. For example, he started prioritizing time with his players to build a stronger team dynamic, rather than overextending himself with external obligations. After stepping away from coaching, Ditka continued this practice by focusing on causes he deeply cared about, like health advocacy and charitable work.

Ditka's journey underscores the importance of learning to say no as a means of preserving energy for what truly matters. His ability to prioritize helped him achieve sustained success, not just in football but in life. His story demonstrates that even in high-pressure, high-profile roles, setting boundaries is essential for long-term achievement and personal well-being.

How to Politely Say No Without Over-Explaining

When declining a request, avoiding over-explaining is crucial. A simple, "I'm not available," is often sufficient. Over-explaining can unintentionally weaken your position and open the door to unnecessary pushback. To politely and effectively say no, follow these steps:

1. **Acknowledge and Appreciate the Offer:**
   Start with gratitude to show respect and consideration. For example:
   - "Thank you for thinking of me, but..."
   - "I really appreciate the invitation, but..."

2. **State Your Reason Briefly:**
   You don't need to give a lengthy explanation. A short and polite reason suffices:
   - "Unfortunately, I'm not able to..."
   - "I'm currently too busy with..."

3. **Offer an Alternative (If Appropriate):**
   If possible, provide an alternative solution or timeline:
   - "I can't do this now, but maybe another time?"
   - "I'm not the right person for this, but I can suggest someone else."

4. **Express Regret While Declining:**
   Acknowledging the situation with regret can soften the decline:
   - "I wish I could, but..."
   - "Sadly, I have something else going on."

5. **Use a Simple "No, Thank You":**
   A straightforward and polite refusal works well in many situations:
   - "No, thank you."
   - "I'll have to pass on this."

6. **Explain Your Priorities (If Needed):**
   If the situation calls for it, briefly explain your commitments:
   - "I need to prioritize my other responsibilities right now."

7. **Ask for Time to Consider:**
   If you're uncertain, buy time to assess your options:
   - "Let me think about it and get back to you."

8. **Be Direct but Kind:**
   A firm but respectful no leaves no room for ambiguity:
   - "I'm going to have to decline this request."

Example Phrases for Saying No Politely

- "I'm flattered, but I can't make it."
- "I'm not available at this time."
- "I'm afraid I have to say no to that."
- "I'm not the best fit for this project."
- "I'll have to take a raincheck on this one."

Key Points to Remember

- **Be Clear and Concise:** Avoid leaving room for misinterpretation.
- **Be Respectful:** Stay courteous and avoid sounding dismissive.
- **Be Honest (When Appropriate):** Share a brief explanation if it adds clarity.
- **Maintain Positive Relationships:** Conclude on a friendly note to preserve goodwill.

By keeping your response simple, respectful, and confident, you set boundaries effectively while maintaining strong relationships and avoiding unnecessary guilt or conflict.

4. Set Boundaries with Draining Individuals: Protecting Your Energy Limit Interaction:

Setting boundaries with individuals who consistently drain your energy is crucial for preserving emotional well-being and maintaining balance in your life. Draining individuals, often referred to as "emotional vampires," can leave you feeling exhausted, anxious, or overwhelmed through excessive negativity, criticism, or demands. While it's not always possible to completely avoid such people—especially if they are family members or colleagues—you can take intentional steps to limit their impact on your mental health. Scheduling interactions for times when you feel mentally strong and prepared ensures you have the emotional capacity to handle their behavior without being overwhelmed.

From a psychological perspective, this approach aligns with the concept of *emotional self-regulation*, which involves managing your emotional responses to maintain balance and resilience. By limiting exposure to draining individuals, you're actively creating space to prioritize your own needs and energy. Strategies such as redirecting conversations, maintaining physical distance, or using polite but firm language to end a discussion can help establish these boundaries. This also involves practicing *assertiveness*, a key skill in boundary-setting, which allows you to communicate your limits clearly and respectfully without guilt or defensiveness.

A real-life example of successfully managing draining relationships is **Eleanor Roosevelt**, who navigated complex family dynamics with grace. As First Lady, she often faced criticism and negativity from those around her, including her domineering mother-in-law, Sara Delano Roosevelt. Eleanor recognized the need to limit the emotional toll of these interactions by setting firm boundaries, focusing on her personal projects, and building a supportive circle of friends and confidants who uplifted her. By doing so, she not only protected her energy but also emerged as a powerful advocate for social change, demonstrating how prioritizing self-care and managing draining relationships can empower personal growth and success.

By setting boundaries with draining individuals, you reclaim your energy and focus on what truly matters in your life. It's not about rejecting people entirely but about creating healthy limits that preserve your emotional resilience. Through clear communication, self-awareness, and deliberate action, you can navigate challenging relationships with confidence and protect your mental well-being.

Protect Your Time: Creating Healthy Boundaries

Protecting your time is an essential part of maintaining emotional balance and preventing burnout, especially when dealing with draining individuals. Time is one of your most valuable resources, and setting limits helps you prioritize your energy for activities and relationships that align with your well-being. For instance, with a draining family member who monopolizes your attention or brings negativity to your day, you can assertively say, "I can only stay for an hour," or, "I need some time to recharge; let's talk another day." By clearly defining the time and energy you are willing to invest, you create a boundary that protects your mental health while maintaining the relationship on your terms.

From a psychological perspective, this aligns with the principles of *time management* and *assertiveness training*. Research has shown that effective time management reduces stress and enhances overall well-being. Similarly, assertiveness empowers individuals to communicate their needs and limits respectfully, fostering healthier interpersonal dynamics. When you protect your time, you're practicing *self-efficacy*—the belief in your ability to influence your circumstances. This reinforces your confidence and reduces feelings of helplessness or resentment that can arise from overextending yourself.

A modern-day example of someone who effectively protects their time is entrepreneur **Arianna Huffington**, founder of *The Huffington Post* and *Thrive Global*. Early in her career, Huffington often overworked herself, leading to exhaustion and burnout. After a health scare, she became an advocate for setting boundaries and prioritizing well-being. She now encourages professionals to protect their time by scheduling breaks, saying no to excessive commitments, and disconnecting from work when needed. Her approach to time management has not only enhanced her personal health but also inspired countless others to adopt healthier habits, proving that protecting your time is a vital step toward long-term success and balance.

By setting clear time limits and communicating them assertively, you show respect for both yourself and the other person. Protecting your time enables you to recharge, focus on what truly matters, and foster healthier, more balanced relationships. It's not about cutting people off but about ensuring that your interactions contribute to your overall well-being rather than detract from it.

Protect Your Time: Safeguarding Your Most Valuable Resource

Time is one of the most precious and non-renewable resources you have, and protecting it is crucial for maintaining balance and well-being. When dealing with draining individuals—such as family members who demand excessive attention or bring negativity into interactions—it's important to set clear and compassionate limits. For example, saying, "I can only stay for an hour," or, "I need some time to recharge; let's talk another day," helps establish boundaries while preserving the relationship. These statements are not just about protecting your time; they are about prioritizing your emotional health and ensuring that your interactions are intentional and manageable.

In psychology, this practice relates to **boundary-setting**, which is essential for emotional self-regulation. Boundaries help you manage stress and prevent resentment by creating a structure for how your time and energy are allocated. It also aligns with the concept of *assertiveness training*, where individuals learn to express their needs and limits clearly and respectfully. By taking control of how you spend your time, you demonstrate self-respect and teach others to value your boundaries, ultimately fostering healthier relationships and interactions.

A relatable example of protecting your time comes from the practice of "time blocking," which many successful professionals use to structure their days. Think of how tech entrepreneur **Elon Musk** schedules his day in five-minute blocks to maximize productivity. While Musk's method may seem extreme, it illustrates the importance of being intentional with time management. On a personal level, setting boundaries with a family member might mean planning a specific timeframe for a visit or a phone call and communicating this in advance. For example, you might say, *"I'd love to catch up, but I can only talk for 20 minutes because I have other commitments."* This approach ensures the interaction is meaningful while preventing it from derailing your other priorities.

Protecting your time isn't about rejecting people or responsibilities—it's about creating space for what truly matters and maintaining control over your energy. By setting clear limits, you empower yourself to engage more positively with others and live in alignment with your values and goals.

Redirect Conversations: Steering Toward Positivity

Redirecting conversations is a powerful tool for maintaining emotional well-being and fostering more productive interactions. When discussions veer into negativity or topics that drain your energy, a polite yet assertive redirection can help shift the focus. Statements like, *"Let's focus on solutions,"* or, *"I'd rather talk about something uplifting,"* gently guide the dialogue away from unproductive or toxic patterns. This approach not only protects your mental energy but also encourages a more constructive and positive atmosphere for everyone involved.

Psychologically, this strategy aligns with the concept of *emotional contagion*—the idea that emotions can spread from one person to another during social interactions. By steering conversations toward uplifting or solution-focused topics, you counteract the spread of negativity and create an environment where optimism and collaboration thrive. Additionally, this technique leverages the principles of **assertiveness training**, enabling individuals to influence the tone of interactions without being confrontational. A well-placed redirection can transform a draining conversation into an opportunity for connection or problem-solving.

A real-life example of this can be seen in the workplace. Imagine a team meeting where a colleague constantly complains about challenges without offering solutions. Instead of letting the negativity dominate, you might say, "I understand this is a challenge, but what are some ideas we can explore to address it?" This response validates their concerns while shifting the focus to proactive problem-solving. Similarly, in personal relationships, redirecting a family member's habitual negativity with a comment like, "I hear you're frustrated; let's talk about something that's been going well lately," can defuse tension and create a more supportive dynamic.

By mastering the art of redirection, you take control of your emotional environment and encourage healthier, more uplifting interactions. This skill not only protects your energy but also inspires others to adopt a more positive and constructive mindset.

Create Work-Specific Boundaries: Protecting Your Professional and Personal Well-Being

Setting boundaries at work is essential for maintaining a healthy balance between professional responsibilities and personal life. One effective strategy is to establish clear availability limits. Communicating when you're accessible for work-related matters—such as saying, *"I'm happy to discuss this during office hours, but I unplug after 6 PM"*—helps define expectations and protects your personal time. This boundary not only ensures you have time to recharge but also fosters respect for your work-life balance among colleagues. Research in psychology highlights the importance of role boundaries, which protect against burnout by preventing work demands from spilling over into personal life. By maintaining these limits, you safeguard your energy and productivity.

Another critical aspect of work-specific boundaries is prioritizing tasks. When faced with an overwhelming workload, communicating your capacity is key to avoiding burnout and ensuring high-quality output. For example, if a manager assigns excessive work, a polite but assertive response like, *"I'd be happy to take this on. Which of my current tasks should I deprioritize?"* allows you to collaborate on managing priorities effectively. This approach is rooted in the psychological concept of assertiveness, which involves expressing your needs and limitations clearly while respecting others' perspectives. Assertive communication helps prevent overcommitment and fosters a more realistic workload, benefiting both you and your team.

A modern example of creating work-specific boundaries can be seen in the practices of LinkedIn **CEO Ryan Roslansky**. In interviews, Roslansky has emphasized the importance of defining work-life boundaries, especially in remote and hybrid work environments. He encourages employees to set "focus hours" where they can work uninterrupted and to disconnect after hours to preserve personal time. Additionally, LinkedIn promotes a culture of delegation and teamwork, empowering employees to share responsibilities and avoid feeling overwhelmed. These practices not only enhance individual well-being but also boost organizational productivity and morale. By setting clear boundaries, prioritizing tasks, and leveraging teamwork, you create a work environment where you can thrive both personally and professionally.

Create Work-Specific Boundaries: Balancing Professional and Personal Demands

Establishing work-specific boundaries is critical for maintaining productivity, preventing burnout, and achieving a healthy work-life balance. One fundamental strategy is setting availability limits. Clearly defining when you are and aren't available for work-related matters, such as stating, *"I'll be glad to go over this tomorrow earlier in the day"* ensures that your personal time is respected. This aligns with the concept of boundary management in psychology, which highlights the need for separating work and personal life to reduce stress. By communicating these limits, you not only protect your downtime but also create an environment where expectations are clear and reasonable.

Prioritizing tasks is another key aspect of maintaining boundaries, especially when workloads become overwhelming. If your manager assigns additional tasks that exceed your capacity, responding assertively with, *"I'd be happy to take this on. Which of my current tasks should I deprioritize?"* demonstrates professionalism and a proactive attitude. This strategy reflects the psychological principle of assertiveness training, which empowers individuals to express their needs while maintaining positive relationships. Prioritizing ensures that your workload remains manageable and allows you to focus on delivering high-quality results rather than being spread too thin.

A modern-day example of setting work-specific boundaries can be found in the remote work culture of companies like **Slack**. Leaders at Slack encourage employees to establish "no-meeting zones" and clearly communicate their availability to foster productivity and well-being. For instance, employees are encouraged to use status indicators to show when they're focused or unavailable and to leverage tools for delegating tasks to team members. This culture of transparency and collaboration helps prevent burnout and creates a healthier work environment. By setting availability limits, prioritizing tasks, and delegating when needed, professionals can maintain their mental health and achieve sustained success in the workplace.

Enforce Boundaries Consistently: Building Trust and Protecting Your Well-Being

Consistently upholding boundaries is crucial to ensuring they are acknowledged and respected. Once you've communicated a boundary, following through on it is critical, as inconsistency can lead to confusion and diminish your credibility. For instance, if you've stated you won't respond to work emails after 6 PM but make exceptions repeatedly, colleagues may assume your boundary isn't firm. Psychology emphasizes the importance of behavioral reinforcement in shaping interactions—when you consistently enforce a boundary, others learn to respect it, reinforcing the behavior you want to see. Upholding boundaries not only protects your well-being but also sets a standard for how you expect to be treated.

Boundaries aren't static; they often need to evolve as circumstances and relationships change. Revisiting and adjusting your boundaries regularly ensures they continue to serve your needs. For example, a parent might adjust work-related boundaries as their child grows older and requires less hands-on attention. Similarly, in friendships or romantic relationships, boundaries may shift to accommodate changes in dynamics or priorities. This aligns with the psychological concept of self-reflection, where individuals evaluate their actions and adapt to maintain alignment with their values and goals. Being open to revisiting boundaries ensures they remain relevant and effective, fostering healthier and more balanced interactions.

By enforcing boundaries with consistency and flexibility, you establish trust and clarity in your relationships. Following through on communicated limits reinforces your self-respect and teaches others to honor your needs. Revisiting and adjusting boundaries as circumstances change ensures they remain aligned with your priorities, creating a foundation for sustainable success and emotional resilience.

Practice Self-Care and Build Resilience: The Key to Sustainable Well-Being

Practicing self-care is fundamental to building resilience and maintaining a healthy balance in life. Regularly recharging through activities that restore your energy, such as exercise, hobbies, or mindfulness practices, helps you stay grounded and better equipped to handle life's challenges. These activities activate the parasympathetic nervous system, which reduces stress and promotes relaxation. For example, mindfulness meditation, a practice backed by psychological research, helps individuals manage stress by fostering self-awareness and emotional regulation. When you prioritize self-care, you create a strong foundation for setting and maintaining boundaries effectively.

Building resilience also involves seeking support from individuals who respect your boundaries and encourage your growth. Surrounding yourself with a positive support system not only reinforces your emotional strength but also provides a safe space for vulnerability and validation. The concept of social support in psychology highlights how meaningful relationships act as a buffer against stress, increasing your capacity to cope with challenges. For example, having a trusted friend or mentor who listens without judgment can make it easier to navigate difficult situations and affirm your decision to prioritize your well-being.

A modern example of these principles in action is tennis star **Naomi Osaka**, who has openly prioritized her mental health and well-being. In 2021, Osaka withdrew from the French Open to focus on her mental health, citing the stress of press obligations and competition. Her decision was met with mixed reactions, but she stood firm, emphasizing the importance of self-care and setting boundaries to protect her mental health. Osaka's actions inspired global conversations about the importance of resilience, self-care, and mental health in high-pressure environments. Her journey demonstrates that practicing self-care, seeking supportive relationships, and being kind to oneself are critical steps toward building resilience and living authentically.

By incorporating self-care practices, cultivating supportive connections, and showing yourself compassion, you can build resilience and navigate life's demands with greater ease. Setting boundaries may feel uncomfortable at first, but acknowledging your progress and treating yourself with kindness helps reinforce your commitment to your well-being and long-term growth.

Conclusion: The Importance of Setting Boundaries for Emotional Well-Being

Setting boundaries is a vital practice for maintaining emotional well-being, managing energy, and fostering healthier relationships. Whether it's limiting exposure to draining individuals, protecting your time, or creating work-specific boundaries, these practices enable you to preserve your mental health and focus on what truly matters. Boundaries act as a framework for self-respect and emotional regulation, helping you navigate life's challenges with clarity and confidence. By consistently enforcing and revisiting these boundaries, you create a sustainable foundation for personal and professional success.

Psychological principles such as emotional self-regulation, assertiveness, and self-reflection reinforce the value of boundaries in everyday interactions. Consistently upholding boundaries not only ensures they are respected but also strengthens your resilience and fosters a greater sense of control over your circumstances. Modern examples, like Naomi Osaka's prioritization of mental health and Arianna Huffington's advocacy for work-life balance, highlight how boundary-setting empowers individuals to protect their well-being, inspire positive change, and achieve long-term fulfillment.

Ultimately, boundaries are not about rejection or isolation—they are about creating healthy limits that honor your needs and values while maintaining respectful relationships. Whether it's redirecting conversations, practicing self-care, or seeking supportive connections, these practices enable you to reclaim your energy, nurture your growth, and live a life aligned with your goals and aspirations.

Key Takeaways

1. Limit Exposure to Draining Individuals: Protect your emotional energy by setting clear boundaries with those who bring negativity into your life.
2. Prioritize Your Time: Define availability limits and focus on tasks and relationships that align with your goals and well-being.
3. Be Assertive and Consistent: Communicate your boundaries clearly and follow through to ensure they are respected.
4. Practice Self-Care: Engage in activities that recharge you and foster resilience.
5. Seek Supportive Connections: Surround yourself with individuals who respect your boundaries and encourage your growth.
6. Revisit and Adjust Boundaries: Adapt your boundaries to reflect changes in your circumstances and priorities.

"Your time is limited, so don't waste it living someone else's life."
– Steve Jobs

CHAPTER 5

Embracing the Unknown: Fear as Fuel for Growth

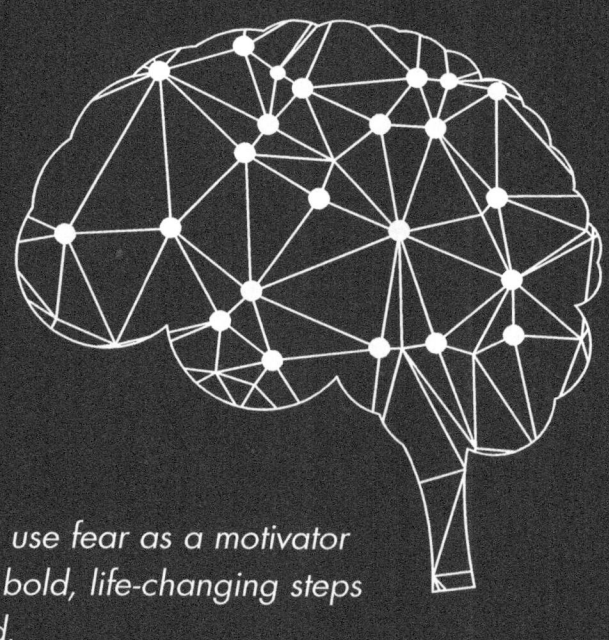

How to use fear as a motivator to take bold, life-changing steps forward.

Harnessing the Power of Fear: Turning Uncertainty into a Catalyst for Growth

Fear of the unknown is a natural human response to uncertainty, but it doesn't have to be a barrier. Instead, it can serve as a powerful motivator for personal growth and transformation. When embraced intentionally, fear can push you out of your comfort zone, unlocking new opportunities and fostering resilience. The key is to reframe your relationship with fear and channel it into purposeful action.

1. Reframing Fear: From Obstacle to Opportunity

Fear is not inherently negative—it's a sign that you're venturing into uncharted territory. Often, fear reflects the significance of what's at stake. For example, you might feel fear when pursuing a career change, starting a new relationship, or launching a business. These fears stem from valuing the potential outcome and not wanting to fail. Instead of avoiding fear, embrace it as evidence of growth. This perspective aligns with the psychological principle of *growth mindset*, which suggests that challenges and setbacks are opportunities to develop rather than indicators of failure. By seeing fear as an ally, you can use it as a signal to push forward rather than retreat.

2. Using Fear to Build Resilience

Resilience, or the ability to bounce back from adversity, is often developed in the face of fear and uncertainty. When you confront fears incrementally, you strengthen your capacity to handle stress and uncertainty. This concept, known as *exposure therapy* in psychology, demonstrates that repeatedly facing fears in manageable doses reduces their intensity over time. For instance, if public speaking makes you anxious, starting with small, informal presentations builds confidence gradually. Each success reinforces your ability to navigate fear, transforming it from a source of anxiety into a foundation for resilience.

In addition, fear triggers the release of adrenaline, sharpening focus and enhancing performance in high-stakes situations. Athletes, for example, often use pre-competition fear to heighten their mental and physical preparedness. Channeling fear into preparation and practice allows you to harness its energy productively rather than letting it paralyze you.

3. Fear as a Compass for Purpose

Fear often points toward what truly matters to you. If something doesn't provoke fear, it likely doesn't hold much personal significance. This is where *value-driven behavior* becomes essential. By identifying the fears associated with your goals, you uncover the values driving them. For instance, fear of failing in a creative endeavor might indicate how deeply you care about expressing yourself. Rather than shying away, use fear to clarify your motivations and take steps that align with your values.

An Inspiring True Story:
The Dalai Lama (Holy Figure)

The Dalai Lama fled Tibet in 1959, fearing for his life and the survival of his people under Chinese rule. Though exiled, he did not allow fear to paralyze him. Instead, he used it as a catalyst for promoting peace, compassion, and Tibetan culture on a global stage. His teachings emphasize mindfulness and acceptance, encouraging people to confront fear with inner peace and understanding. The Dalai Lama's journey illustrates that even in the face of immense uncertainty, fear can guide us toward greater resilience and purpose.

A Real-Life Example: Sara Blakely

Sara Blakely, the founder of Spanx, turned fear into fuel on her journey to building a billion-dollar brand. Early in her career, Blakely faced rejection after rejection while pitching her product. Instead of letting fear of failure paralyze her, she reframed it as part of the process of achieving something great. Blakely often cites her father's influence, as he encouraged her to celebrate failures as learning opportunities. This perspective helped her embrace uncertainty and take bold steps forward, such as cold-calling manufacturers and meeting with department store executives.

Blakely also used fear as a motivator to prepare thoroughly. Recognizing her lack of experience in business, she immersed herself in learning, studied her industry, and persisted through challenges. Her willingness to embrace fear and take risks led to Spanx's incredible success, proving that fear, when harnessed effectively, can be a catalyst for growth.

Strategies for Harnessing Fear:
Acknowledging and Accepting Fear: A Path to Growth

Fear is a natural and universal human emotion, often arising in the face of uncertainty or significant change. Recognizing fear as a normal part of life, rather than a weakness, is a critical first step toward managing it effectively. Psychologically, fear serves an evolutionary purpose, alerting us to potential dangers or challenges. However, in modern life, fear often stems from perceived threats, such as the possibility of failure, rejection, or the unknown. Acknowledging the presence of fear reduces its emotional grip, allowing individuals to approach challenges with clarity and resilience. By naming the fear—such as saying, *"I'm afraid of failing at this presentation"*—you bring it into the open, making it easier to address and reframe.

This approach aligns with the psychological concept of ***emotional labeling***, which suggests that naming emotions reduces their intensity by engaging the prefrontal cortex, the brain's rational thinking center. Instead of being overwhelmed by fear, individuals can analyze it, understand its source, and develop strategies to move forward. Accepting fear does not mean surrendering to it; rather, it involves embracing it as a natural response that can coexist with courage. When fear is acknowledged, it becomes a stepping stone rather than a stumbling block, encouraging growth and action.

A modern-day example is actor **Emma Stone**, who has openly discussed her struggle with severe anxiety and panic attacks during her childhood.

Instead of letting fear dictate her life, Stone acknowledged her anxiety and sought therapy to better understand and manage it. Her therapist encouraged her to name and confront her fears, which empowered her to take small, deliberate steps toward her passion for acting. Over time, what initially terrified her—performing in front of others—became her greatest strength. Today, Stone not only excels in her craft but also uses her platform to raise awareness about mental health, proving that acknowledging and accepting fear can lead to extraordinary personal and professional growth.

By naming and accepting fear, individuals create space for self-awareness and constructive action. Fear, when acknowledged, loses its ability to paralyze and instead becomes a source of insight and motivation. This shift in perspective allows people to approach challenges with greater confidence, fostering resilience and unlocking their full potential.

Shifting Perspective: Turning Fear into an Opportunity

Fear is often perceived as a barrier, signaling danger or failure. However, reframing fear as a signal of opportunity can transform it into a powerful motivator. Psychologically, fear arises from the brain's amygdala, which triggers the fight-or-flight response. While this response is essential for survival, it can also misinterpret challenges as threats. By shifting perspective, individuals can recognize fear as a sign that they're stepping into uncharted territory—an area where growth and progress often occur. This reframing aligns with the concept of *growth mindset*, which encourages embracing challenges as opportunities to learn and improve.

Reframing fear requires identifying the positive possibilities hidden within it. For instance, fear of public speaking can be seen not as a barrier but as an opportunity to share ideas, connect with others, and build confidence. This cognitive restructuring, a technique from **cognitive-behavioral therapy (CBT)**, involves challenging negative thought patterns and replacing them with empowering beliefs. Instead of saying, "I'm going to fail," one might think, "This is a chance to gain experience and grow." This shift reduces fear's intensity and allows individuals to focus on the potential benefits rather than the risks.

A modern example of shifting perspective is **Alex Honnold**, the professional rock climber who famously scaled El Capitan without ropes in the documentary ***Free Solo***. While fear was a constant presence during his preparation, Honnold reframed it as a signal to prepare meticulously. He used fear to drive his training, honing his skills, memorizing every move, and visualizing success. Rather than letting fear paralyze him, he saw it as an opportunity to challenge his limits and achieve something extraordinary. His accomplishment not only demonstrated physical prowess but also the power of a reframed mindset to turn fear into a catalyst for greatness. Alex Honnold's journey perfectly encapsulates the raw tension between fear and the drive for mastery. His ability to remain calm, calculated, and committed while facing such extreme risks is both inspiring and nerve-wracking.

By shifting perspective and viewing fear as an indicator of opportunity, individuals can move from avoidance to action. This mindset fosters resilience, enabling people to face challenges with confidence and determination. Ultimately, reframing fear allows for personal growth, transforming what once seemed like a barrier into a stepping stone toward success. The wisdom is profound: crises can become opportunities when approached with resilience and creativity.

Acting Despite Fear: Building Momentum Through Small Steps

Fear often triggers a natural inclination to avoid or freeze, but taking action, even in small increments, is one of the most effective ways to overcome it. This approach aligns with the psychological concept of *behavioral activation*, which emphasizes the importance of engaging in meaningful activities to combat fear or anxiety. Starting small allows individuals to build confidence and momentum, transforming fear from a paralyzing force into a manageable challenge. Each step, no matter how minor, reinforces the belief that progress is possible and fear can be faced and overcome.

Incremental progress is crucial because it prevents overwhelm. Breaking a daunting goal into smaller, actionable tasks reduces the perceived risk and makes the path forward clearer. For instance, someone afraid of public speaking might begin by practicing in front of a mirror, then progress to presenting to a small group of friends, and finally to a larger audience. This method, rooted in ***graded exposure therapy***, is used in psychology to gradually desensitize individuals to fear-inducing situations. With each successful step, the brain rewires itself to associate the feared activity with positive outcomes, making future actions easier and less intimidating.

A modern example of acting despite fear is the story of **Shonda Rhimes**, the acclaimed television producer and writer behind *Grey's Anatomy* and *Scandal*. In her book *Year of Yes*, Rhimes shares how fear held her back from embracing opportunities outside her comfort zone. Determined to change, she began saying "yes" to things that scared her, such as public speaking or attending social events. She started small, focusing on manageable challenges, and each successful experience built her confidence to tackle bigger fears. Over time, her incremental actions transformed her life, expanding her professional and personal horizons in ways she never imagined.

By taking small steps and focusing on consistent progress, individuals can break free from the paralysis of fear. Every action builds momentum, fostering a sense of accomplishment and resilience. Acting despite fear not only diminishes its power but also opens doors to opportunities for growth and transformation, proving that **courage is not the absence of fear but the decision to move forward anyway.**

Seeking Support: The Power of Connection in Navigating Uncertainty

When navigating uncertainty, seeking support from encouraging and uplifting sources is essential for maintaining emotional resilience. Human beings are inherently social creatures, and connection with others has a profound impact on mental health. Supportive relationships provide a safe space to share fears, gain perspective, and receive encouragement during challenging times. Whether it's trusted friends, family, colleagues, or even pets, having a reliable support system helps individuals feel understood and less isolated, fostering a sense of stability and belonging.

From a psychological perspective, this concept aligns with social support theory, which emphasizes the benefits of emotional, informational, and instrumental support. Emotional support involves empathy and reassurance, while informational support provides guidance and advice, and instrumental support includes tangible help, like assistance with tasks. Additionally, interacting with pets offers unique emotional benefits, as studies have shown that pets can reduce stress, lower blood pressure, and promote feelings of comfort and unconditional love. By leaning on a diverse support system, individuals can draw strength from multiple sources, creating a robust foundation for resilience.

A surprising example of the power of seeking support is actor **Dwayne "The Rock" Johnson**, who has openly discussed the importance of his support system in navigating personal and professional challenges. Johnson has credited his family and friends with helping him through periods of depression and uncertainty early in his career. He also highlights the comfort and stability he derives from his dogs, often sharing how their presence lifts his spirits. By surrounding himself with uplifting people and pets, Johnson has been able to stay grounded and focused, even during times of immense pressure and uncertainty. His journey exemplifies how seeking support fosters emotional strength and enables individuals to persevere through life's challenges.

By seeking support, individuals cultivate a sense of connection and empowerment, which is crucial when facing the unknown. Encouragement from others reinforces confidence, while pets offer a unique form of companionship and stress relief. Together, these relationships create a network of strength, allowing individuals to navigate uncertainty with greater ease and resilience.

Breaking Down Goals: Building Confidence Through Incremental Steps

Breaking down large, intimidating goals into smaller, manageable steps is a proven strategy for overcoming fear and building confidence. When faced with a daunting task, fear often arises from the overwhelming scope of the challenge. By tackling goals in smaller increments, individuals can focus on immediate, achievable actions rather than the entire journey, making the process less intimidating. This approach reduces the likelihood of procrastination and helps create a sense of accomplishment, which motivates continued progress.

This concept aligns with the psychological principle of **successive approximation**, a technique often used in behavioral psychology. Successive approximation involves gradually approaching a desired behavior or goal by reinforcing small steps along the way. Each incremental success builds a sense of competence and reinforces positive behavior, encouraging individuals to take the next step. For example, someone fearful of public speaking might start by practicing in front of a mirror, then progress to speaking in front of a trusted friend, and eventually to larger audiences. Each step reduces anxiety and builds confidence, transforming the once-daunting goal into an achievable reality.

A recent example of breaking down goals can be found in the journey of fitness influencer **Joe Wicks**, also known as **"The Body Coach."** During the COVID-19 pandemic, Wicks aimed to keep people active by creating a global fitness initiative through online classes. While his goal of reaching millions worldwide might have seemed overwhelming, he approached it incrementally. Wicks started with daily live-streamed workouts targeted at children stuck at home, gradually expanding to include families and broader audiences. By focusing on one workout at a time and celebrating small milestones, he not only achieved his goal but also became a global fitness icon, inspiring millions to prioritize their health.

Breaking goals into smaller steps also mitigates the fear of failure, as it reduces the stakes for each action. Rather than risking a major setback, incremental progress provides opportunities for learning and adjustment, fostering a growth-oriented mindset. This perspective aligns with self-efficacy theory by psychologist Albert Bandura, which emphasizes that confidence grows when individuals see their actions leading to tangible results. Success in small tasks reinforces the belief in one's ability to handle larger challenges, creating a cycle of empowerment.

By tackling goals in small, incremental steps, individuals can transform fear into actionable momentum. Each step builds confidence, reduces anxiety, and creates a sense of achievement, making it easier to confront challenges head-on. This method not only makes intimidating goals more manageable but also fosters resilience, empowering individuals to embrace growth and accomplish their aspirations.

Reflecting on Success: Strengthening Confidence Through Past Achievements

Reflecting on past successes is a powerful way to reinforce confidence and resilience when facing fear or uncertainty. By revisiting moments where you overcame challenges, you remind yourself of your capabilities and resourcefulness. This practice taps into the psychological concept of **self-efficacy**, developed by **Albert Bandura**, which highlights how belief in one's ability to succeed influences motivation and performance. When individuals recall instances of overcoming fear, they reframe their self-image as capable and courageous, fostering the confidence needed to tackle future challenges.

Reflection is not merely about basking in past victories but about understanding the strategies and mindsets that contributed to success. Identifying patterns, such as persistence, creative problem-solving, or support from others, provides a roadmap for navigating current fears. For example, someone who overcame the fear of starting a new job by seeking mentorship and preparing thoroughly can apply the same approach when facing future professional challenges. This process strengthens the neural pathways associated with positive experiences, making it easier to draw on those feelings of accomplishment during stressful times.

A historical example of overcoming fear and reflecting on success is

Franklin D. Roosevelt (FDR). Faced with personal adversity after contracting polio, FDR feared his political career might be over. However, he approached his rehabilitation with determination, learning to manage his physical limitations and build emotional resilience. Later, as President of the United States during the Great Depression and World War II, FDR's famous statement, *"The only thing we have to fear is fear itself,"* reflected his personal philosophy. His ability to reflect on his own triumphs over adversity allowed him to inspire confidence in a nation facing unprecedented challenges. Looking back on how he overcame his fears shaped his leadership, demonstrating the power of reflection in reinforcing resilience.

For those looking to reprogram their minds using **Neuro-Linguistic Programming (NLP)** techniques, reflection plays a central role. NLP emphasizes identifying limiting beliefs and replacing them with empowering ones. Techniques like **anchoring**—where you associate a physical gesture or word with a positive memory—can help reinforce feelings of confidence when reflecting on past successes. For instance, recalling a time you overcame fear and pairing that memory with a specific word or gesture can create a mental shortcut to that positive state. Another NLP technique, **visualization**, involves vividly replaying successful moments in your mind, amplifying the emotions and lessons learned to make them more accessible in future situations.

By regularly reflecting on past successes, individuals can harness the psychological benefits of self-efficacy and rewire their minds to approach fear with confidence. Whether through historical examples like FDR, personal reflection, or NLP techniques, the act of looking back reminds us of our inherent strength and ability to grow. This practice not only bolsters resilience but also provides a blueprint for overcoming future challenges.

Prepare Thoroughly: Overcoming Fear with Confidence

Fear often arises from the unknown, where uncertainty breeds doubt and hesitation. Thorough preparation is one of the most effective strategies for overcoming this fear, as it reduces uncertainty and instills a sense of control.

When you prepare meticulously, you replace guesswork with knowledge and readiness, giving yourself the tools to face challenges with confidence. Preparation also aligns with the psychological concept of proactive coping, which involves anticipating potential stressors and taking steps to mitigate their impact. By focusing on what you can control, you shift your mindset from fear to empowerment.

In addition to reducing uncertainty, preparation fosters mental toughness, the ability to remain resilient and composed under pressure. Mental toughness is cultivated through repeated exposure to challenging situations where preparation plays a critical role. For instance, a well-prepared individual is better equipped to handle unexpected outcomes because their groundwork provides a solid foundation for adaptive problem-solving. This approach not only builds confidence but also enhances performance, as the mind is less distracted by anxiety and more focused on execution.

An interesting example of thorough preparation and mental toughness is **Mark Zuckerberg**, who earned his black belt in Brazilian Jiu-Jitsu while managing his responsibilities as CEO of Meta. Brazilian Jiu-Jitsu is a sport that requires strategy, adaptability, and focus—qualities Zuckerberg consistently brings to his professional life. His commitment to training highlights the importance of preparation in mastering both physical and mental challenges. By immersing himself in rigorous training and embracing the discipline of martial arts, Zuckerberg has showcased how preparation reduces fear, sharpens decision-making, and builds resilience.

For those looking to enhance their preparation using **Neuro-Linguistic Programming (NLP)** techniques, visualization and reframing are particularly effective tools. Visualization involves mentally rehearsing a task or situation in vivid detail, imagining yourself performing successfully. This technique creates neural pathways in the brain, making the actual task feel familiar and less intimidating. For example, if you're preparing for a public speech, visualize yourself speaking confidently, engaging the audience, and handling questions with ease. **Reframing**, another NLP technique, involves shifting your perception of a challenge. Instead of viewing preparation as a tedious task, you can reframe it as an opportunity to equip yourself with the confidence and skills needed to excel.

By preparing thoroughly, individuals can tackle fear with a clear mind and greater confidence. Whether through rigorous training like Zuckerberg, psychological techniques, or NLP strategies, preparation reduces uncertainty and transforms fear into actionable determination. This proactive approach empowers individuals to face challenges with resilience and clarity, proving that success begins long before the moment of execution.

Celebrate Small Wins: Reinforcing Growth Through Progress

Celebrating small wins is a powerful tool for overcoming fear and building momentum toward success. Each time you face fear and take action, acknowledging even the smallest progress reinforces positive behavior, strengthening your confidence and resilience. Psychologically, this concept aligns with the principle of ***positive reinforcement***, where rewarding desirable actions encourages their repetition. When individuals take the time to reflect on their progress, they activate the brain's reward system, releasing dopamine—a neurotransmitter associated with motivation and pleasure. This chemical boost not only enhances mood but also fosters a stronger drive to continue tackling challenges.

Recognizing small victories is particularly important when dealing with fear, as it shifts focus from what remains to be done to what has already been accomplished. This perspective helps reframe fear as a manageable and temporary obstacle rather than an insurmountable barrier. Celebrating incremental progress also aligns with ***self-efficacy theory***, which emphasizes that confidence grows when individuals experience success in smaller, achievable tasks. For instance, someone afraid of public speaking might celebrate completing a short presentation to a small group, building confidence for larger audiences in the future.

A remarkable example of celebrating small wins and overcoming fear is the story of **Harland Sanders**, better known as **Colonel Sanders**, the founder of KFC. At the age of 65, Sanders faced a series of personal and professional failures, including the closure of his roadside restaurant due to the construction of a new interstate. Instead of giving in to fear and defeat, he decided to start anew, taking his fried chicken recipe on the road. Sanders faced countless rejections while pitching his franchise concept to restaurants, but each small victory—securing even one partnership—reinforced his belief in his product and vision. Over time, those small wins snowballed into the creation of a global fast-food empire.

Sanders' story highlights how celebrating small victories can reprogram the mind to overcome fear and persist through setbacks. By focusing on progress rather than failure, Sanders was able to rebuild his confidence and resilience. This mindset shift aligns with *cognitive-behavioral techniques* used in psychology, such as *reframing negative thoughts*. Sanders didn't dwell on the 1,000-plus rejections he faced but instead celebrated each successful step, using those moments as motivation to keep going. This approach demonstrates how incremental progress can reshape perceptions of fear and failure, paving the way for transformative success.

For those seeking to reprogram their mindset, techniques from *Neuro-Linguistic Programming (NLP)* can be highly effective. For example, **anchoring** involves associating a physical gesture or phrase with positive feelings of accomplishment. By recalling past wins and pairing them with an anchor, individuals can recreate the confidence and motivation needed to face future fears. **Visualization**, another NLP strategy, involves imagining each small victory leading toward a larger goal. These practices not only help individuals embrace fear but also encourage them to celebrate their progress, reinforcing the belief that success is achievable.

Celebrating small wins creates a cycle of motivation and growth, turning fear into fuel for progress. Like Harland Sanders, individuals can overcome setbacks and reframe failure as part of the journey. By acknowledging incremental achievements, embracing positive reinforcement, and employing techniques like NLP, anyone can reprogram their mind to persist in the face of fear, ultimately achieving success and fulfillment in life's endeavors.

Embracing Fear and Celebrating Small Wins: A Conclusion

Fear is often seen as a barrier to progress, but when approached intentionally, it becomes a powerful motivator and a guide for growth. Acknowledging and confronting fear allows individuals to transform it from a source of paralysis into a catalyst for action. Celebrating small wins along the way reinforces positive behavior and builds resilience, turning daunting challenges into manageable and rewarding journeys. This process is not about achieving perfection but about recognizing and valuing incremental progress, which fosters a sense of accomplishment and strengthens confidence.

Psychologically, celebrating small wins aligns with the principles of positive reinforcement and self-efficacy. Each achievement, no matter how minor, activates the brain's reward system, creating a feedback loop that enhances motivation and commitment. By focusing on what has been accomplished rather than what remains to be done, individuals can reframe their perception of fear and gain momentum toward their goals. The story of Harland Sanders exemplifies this: despite facing repeated failures and rejections, he celebrated each small victory, using them as stepping stones to create the global KFC franchise. His journey underscores the transformative power of persistence and the importance of embracing fear as part of the growth process.

To further reprogram the mind and harness fear effectively, techniques like Neuro-Linguistic Programming (NLP) provide practical tools. Anchoring positive emotions to physical gestures or phrases, visualizing incremental successes, and reframing negative thoughts are all strategies that empower individuals to build confidence and resilience. These practices not only help individuals overcome fear but also encourage them to celebrate their progress, reinforcing the belief that success is achievable through consistent effort and determination. Fear, when viewed as an ally rather than an adversary, becomes a guiding force toward personal fulfillment and transformative success.

Key Takeaways

1. **Acknowledge Fear:** Recognize fear as a normal part of growth and view it as a sign that you are pushing beyond your comfort zone.
2. **Celebrate Small Wins:** Acknowledge and reward incremental progress to build confidence and sustain motivation.
3. **Reframe Fear:** Shift your perspective to see fear as an opportunity for growth and a signal of what truly matters.
4. **Leverage Positive Reinforcement:** Use psychological strategies, like positive reinforcement and self-efficacy, to foster resilience and perseverance.
5. **Employ NLP Techniques:** Practice anchoring, visualization, and reframing to reprogram your mind and cultivate a success-oriented mindset.
6. **Learn from Examples:** Draw inspiration from figures like Harland Sanders, who turned failures into opportunities by celebrating small victories and persisting despite fear.

By embracing fear, celebrating progress, and utilizing effective mental strategies, individuals can unlock their potential and turn challenges into triumphs, paving the way for meaningful success in life.

"Courage is resistance to fear, mastery of fear-not absence of fear.
— Mark Twain

CHAPTER 6

Creating a Vision for Your Life

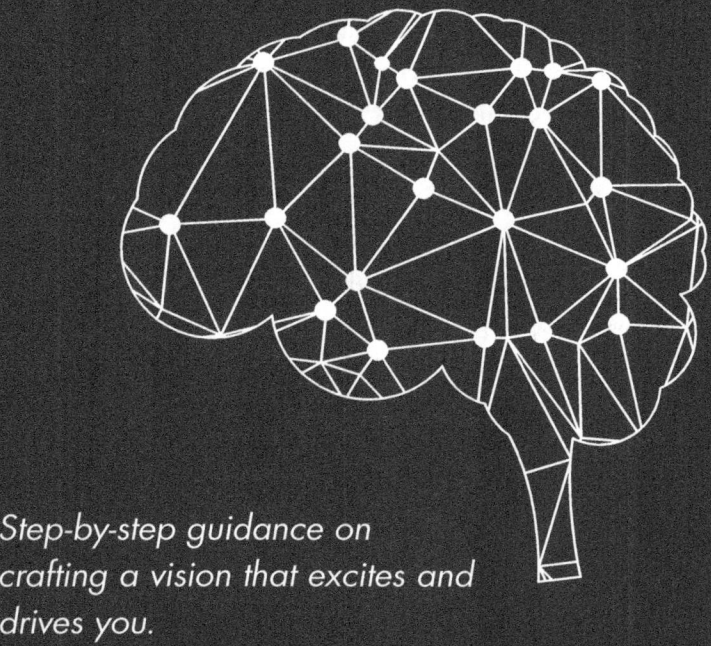

Step-by-step guidance on crafting a vision that excites and drives you.

Crafting a vision for your life is one of the most powerful steps you can take to align your actions with your aspirations and create a sense of purpose. A vision serves as a guiding star, providing clarity and motivation as you navigate life's complexities. It begins with introspection: reflecting on your values, passions, and the impact you want to make in the world. When you connect with what truly matters to you, your vision becomes deeply personal and meaningful, driving you forward with enthusiasm and resilience.

Visualization is a critical tool in shaping this vision. The process involves imagining your ideal future in vivid detail, engaging all your senses to make the experience feel real. **Neuro-Linguistic Programming (NLP)** offers techniques such as **mental rehearsal** and **anchoring**, which can amplify the effectiveness of visualization. For example, picture yourself in a future scenario where you've achieved your goals—what does it look like, feel like, and sound like? This exercise helps your brain create a mental blueprint, priming it to recognize opportunities and take actions that align with your aspirations.

Once you have a clear picture of your vision, it's essential to break it down into actionable steps. A vision without a plan can feel overwhelming, but setting specific, achievable goals makes it tangible. Use techniques like **SMART goals**—ensuring your objectives are Specific, Measurable, Achievable, Relevant, and Time-bound. For example, if your vision involves starting a business, outline steps such as researching your market, developing a product, and creating a timeline for launch. Each milestone you achieve reinforces your belief in your vision, building momentum and confidence.

Finally, a compelling vision isn't just about personal success—it often includes contributing to something greater than yourself. Whether it's improving your community, inspiring others, or leaving a legacy, integrating a broader purpose into your vision gives it depth and sustainability. Surround yourself with supportive individuals who share or respect your aspirations, as their encouragement and insights can help you stay focused and resilient. By creating a vision rooted in authenticity, supported by action, and infused with purpose, you'll unlock the motivation and clarity needed to achieve a fulfilling life.

Crafting a Vision for Life Using NLP, Manifesting, and Visualization

Creating a compelling vision for life is a transformative process that leverages the principles of Neuro-Linguistic Programming (NLP), manifesting, and visualization to align your thoughts, emotions, and actions toward success. Below is a step-by-step guide designed to inspire, energize, and empower you to reach your goals in life and business.

Step 1: Clarify Your Desired Future

What to Do:

- Reflect deeply on what success and fulfillment mean to you. Ask yourself questions like:
  - *What would my ideal day look like?*
  - *What am I passionate about?*
  - *What legacy do I want to leave behind?*
- Write down specific, measurable, and inspiring goals for different areas of life (career, relationships, health, personal growth, and contribution).

NLP Technique:

- Outcome Framing: Use the SMART (Specific, Measurable, Achievable, Relevant, Time-bound) framework to define goals. For example, instead of saying, "I want to be successful," say, "I want to grow my business to $500,000 in annual revenue by December 2026."

Step 2: Use Visualization to Imagine Success

What to Do:

- Close your eyes and create a vivid mental image of your ideal future. Include as much sensory detail as possible:
  ☼ *What do you see, hear, feel, smell, and taste in your vision of success?*
- Visualize the process, not just the outcome. Imagine yourself taking the necessary steps confidently and joyfully.

Manifestation Technique:

- Emotional Alignment: While visualizing, evoke the emotions of already having achieved your goal (joy, gratitude, pride). Your subconscious mind works best when it connects to strong emotions.

Example Exercise:

- If your goal is to own a successful café, picture yourself interacting with happy customers, smelling fresh coffee, hearing laughter, and feeling the satisfaction of running a thriving business.

Step 3: Reprogram Limiting Beliefs

What to Do:

- Identify and challenge any negative beliefs that conflict with your vision (e.g., "I'm not good enough," or "Success is too hard to achieve").
- Replace limiting beliefs with empowering affirmations, such as:
  ○ "I am capable of achieving my dreams."
  ○ "Success comes naturally to me."

NLP Technique:

- Swish Pattern: Imagine the limiting belief as a small, dull image in your mind. Replace it with a bright, empowering image of you succeeding. Repeat this until the limiting belief feels weak and the empowering belief dominates.

Step 4: Take Inspired Action

What to Do:

- Break down your vision into actionable steps and prioritize them.
- Commit to taking at least one small action every day that aligns with your vision.

Manifestation Insight:

- The law of attraction works best when paired with action. As you take steps, you demonstrate commitment, creating opportunities and momentum.

Example Exercise:

- If your vision is to write a book, start with small, achievable goals like writing 500 words a day or outlining one chapter each week.

Step 5: Anchor Your Vision in Your Subconscious Mind

What to Do:

- Use affirmations and visualization daily to reinforce your vision.
- Create a vision board with images, quotes, and symbols representing your goals. Place it where you'll see it often.

NLP Technique:

- Anchoring: Create a physical trigger (e.g., clenching your fist or touching your heart) while visualizing your success. Repeating this strengthens the association between the trigger and the positive emotions of achieving your vision.

Step 6: Monitor Progress and Celebrate Wins

What to Do:

- Reflect regularly on your progress and celebrate small milestones to build confidence and motivation.
- Adjust your plan as needed, ensuring it remains aligned with your core values and evolving desires.

Manifestation Insight:

- Gratitude amplifies positive energy. Daily, write down 3 things you're grateful for that align with your vision, even if they're small.

Step 7: Embrace Resilience and Adaptability

What to Do:

- Treat obstacles as building blocks for success. Adopt a growth mindset and learn from setbacks.
- Use techniques like journaling or meditation to stay centered during tough times.

The Greatest Visionary in World History

Throughout history, countless individuals have shaped the course of humanity with their extraordinary visions. While it's impossible to definitively crown the greatest visionary, certain figures stand out for their unparalleled influence on society, science, and human progress. Among them, **Leonardo da Vinci** often emerges as a quintessential example of a visionary whose ideas transcended his time, laying the groundwork for fields ranging from art to technology. Da Vinci's insatiable curiosity and ability to bridge disciplines epitomize the essence of visionary thinking, making him a timeless symbol of human potential.

Leonardo da Vinci's brilliance lay not only in his art but also in his ability to conceptualize ideas far ahead of his era. From the design of flying machines to detailed anatomical studies, his notebooks are filled with inventions and observations that prefigured modern engineering, medicine, and aviation. What set da Vinci apart was his capacity to think holistically, connecting seemingly unrelated fields to create innovative solutions. His visionary approach wasn't confined to imagining what could be; he meticulously studied the natural world, ensuring his ideas were rooted in practicality. His masterpiece, the *Vitruvian Man*, symbolized the harmony between science and art, reflecting his belief in the interconnectedness of all knowledge.

What makes a visionary truly transformative is the ability to inspire others to dream beyond the confines of their reality. Da Vinci's legacy has influenced countless innovators, from engineers to artists, who have drawn inspiration from his unrelenting curiosity and boundless creativity. His ideas served as a foundation for technological advancements, such as the helicopter and modern robotics, centuries after his death. This enduring impact demonstrates how a visionary's contributions can ripple through time, igniting progress long after their own era.

While many figures could vie for the title of the greatest visionary—such as Albert Einstein for his revolutionary insights into physics or Mahatma Gandhi for his transformative vision of nonviolence—Leonardo da Vinci stands out for his ability to envision a future that seamlessly integrated art, science, and humanity. His life exemplifies how a relentless pursuit of knowledge, combined with imagination and interdisciplinary thinking, can redefine what is possible. Da Vinci's story reminds us that visionaries are not just dreamers; they are architects of the future, whose ideas shape the trajectory of human history.

Harnessing Resources to Shape Beliefs and Reality

Shaping your beliefs and reality to craft a compelling vision for your life requires leveraging a variety of resources, both internal and external. Internal resources include self-awareness, mindfulness, and the ability to reframe negative thoughts into empowering ones. Cognitive-behavioral techniques, such as identifying and challenging limiting beliefs, can help individuals replace self-doubt with self-assurance. Externally, access to mentors, supportive communities, inspirational content, and tools like vision boards or guided meditations can be transformative. Surrounding yourself with individuals who model resilience and success reinforces the belief that change is possible and fosters a growth-oriented mindset.

Psychologically, this process is closely tied to self-efficacy—the belief in one's ability to succeed in specific situations. People with strong self-efficacy are more likely to persevere through challenges and see setbacks as opportunities to learn and grow. Techniques like visualization, used in sports psychology, can help individuals mentally rehearse their desired future, building neural pathways that make those outcomes feel achievable. Manifestation practices, often misunderstood, rely on aligning daily actions with one's aspirations, turning abstract desires into actionable plans.

One modern example of someone who transformed a difficult life through the power of imagination and resilience is **George Foreman's** transformation from a world champion boxer to a successful entrepreneur and is another example of how vision can reshape one's life. Known for his fierce reputation in the boxing ring, Foreman experienced a significant low point after his loss to Muhammad Ali in the iconic "Rumble in the Jungle" fight. The defeat, coupled with other personal struggles, left Foreman searching for purpose beyond boxing. His eventual pivot came after a spiritual awakening, which led him to leave the sport temporarily to become a minister and focus on helping others.

Years later, Foreman returned to boxing, defying the odds by reclaiming the heavyweight title at the age of 45, making him the oldest champion in the sport's history. But his vision extended beyond the ring. Using his newfound fame, Foreman launched the George Foreman Grill, a product that became a global sensation and a symbol of his reinvention. His entrepreneurial success allowed him to support philanthropic efforts and provide for his family in ways he had never imagined.

Foreman's story demonstrates the psychological concept of resilience, the ability to bounce back from setbacks and reinvent oneself. It also highlights how aligning one's actions with personal values and purpose can lead to unexpected opportunities. Like Carver, Foreman's life showcases the transformative power of vision, determination, and a willingness to embrace reinvention in the face of adversity.

Resources to shape beliefs and reality include self-help books, podcasts, online courses, and communities focused on personal development. Examples such **as Tony Robbins'** teachings on personal transformation or **Eckhart Tolle's** guidance on mindfulness provide actionable frameworks for change. By combining these tools with self-reflection, visualization, and consistent effort, individuals can reshape their beliefs, rewrite their narrative, and create a vision that not only transforms their own lives but also positively impacts those around them.

George Washington Carver: Turning Hardship into Visionary Success

George Washington Carver's life epitomizes the power of vision and determination to transform personal hardship into a lasting legacy of innovation and service. Born into slavery during the Civil War and orphaned as a child, Carver faced immense challenges, including systemic racism and a lack of access to education. Despite these barriers, he developed an unshakable belief in the power of knowledge and its potential to uplift communities. He envisioned a future where agriculture, science, and education could be used to empower impoverished farmers and rebuild struggling economies.

Carver's vision was deeply rooted in service and sustainability. He studied agricultural science and became a pioneer in promoting crop rotation and the use of alternative crops, such as peanuts and sweet potatoes, to improve soil health and diversify farming practices. His innovations not only revolutionized agriculture in the southern United States but also provided struggling farmers with tools to escape poverty. Carver's impact extended beyond his technical contributions; his humility, spiritual devotion, and belief in the potential of humanity made him a source of inspiration for generations.

Psychologically, Carver's journey highlights the concept **of post-traumatic growth**, where individuals overcome significant adversity to achieve transformative personal and societal contributions. His ability to envision a brighter future, coupled with a relentless work ethic, demonstrates how aligning one's beliefs with purposeful action can overcome even the most daunting obstacles. Carver's life shows that a clear vision and commitment to service can reshape both personal and collective realities.

Finally, a compelling vision isn't just about personal success—it often includes contributing to something greater than yourself. Whether it's improving your community, inspiring others, or leaving a legacy, integrating a broader purpose into your vision gives it depth and sustainability. Surround yourself with supportive individuals who share or respect your aspirations, as their encouragement and insights can help you stay focused and resilient. By creating a vision rooted in authenticity, supported by action, and infused with purpose, you'll unlock the motivation and clarity needed to achieve a fulfilling life.

Many famous individuals use their influence and resources to contribute to causes greater than themselves, leaving a lasting impact on their communities and the world. **Jon Bon Jovi** is a shining example of this philanthropic spirit. Through his Soul Kitchen restaurants, Bon Jovi offers a "pay-what-you-can" dining model where anyone, regardless of financial circumstances, can enjoy a meal. Those who can't pay in money are encouraged to volunteer their time instead. This innovative approach fosters dignity and community, creating a space where people feel supported and connected. Bon Jovi's efforts reflect a commitment to addressing hunger and homelessness, issues often overlooked despite their prevalence.

Another iconic figure deeply rooted in community service is **Michael Jordan**. Known for his legendary basketball career, Jordan has consistently used his platform to make a difference off the court. His $100 million pledge over ten years to organizations fighting racial inequality and promoting social justice is a testament to his dedication. Jordan also supports initiatives focused on education, such as scholarships for underprivileged students, and healthcare, including funding clinics in underserved communities. His efforts demonstrate a belief in empowering individuals and addressing systemic barriers, ensuring that his legacy transcends sports.

Celebrities in Action: Making the World Better

Actors, musicians, and athletes often leverage their fame for philanthropic endeavors that resonate with their personal values. For example, **Rihanna's** Clara Lionel Foundation focuses on global education and emergency relief efforts. The foundation has funded millions in scholarships and disaster recovery initiatives, particularly in underserved regions. Rihanna's hands-on involvement shows how celebrities can use their platforms to drive meaningful change, addressing urgent issues that impact vulnerable populations.

Anchoring Fame in Giving Back

Philanthropy is not limited to celebrities in the entertainment industry. Athletes like **LeBron James** and **Serena Williams** have also anchored their legacies in giving back. James's "I PROMISE School" in Akron, Ohio, is an ambitious project aimed at providing underprivileged students with a supportive and resource-rich educational environment. The school offers free tuition, meals, transportation, and even college scholarships, showing a holistic approach to tackling the barriers that many children face.

Similarly, Serena Williams has been an advocate for women's equality and education, funding scholarships and championing access to sports for girls in underserved areas.

These efforts are not only acts of charity but also demonstrate how fame can be a powerful force for good. By using their platforms to highlight critical issues, these celebrities inspire others to contribute to causes they are passionate about, amplifying the impact of their work.

The Ripple Effect of Philanthropy

Celebrities like Jon Bon Jovi, Michael Jordan, and others exemplify how fame can be a tool for positive change. Their work fosters a ripple effect, inspiring fans, businesses, and fellow celebrities to contribute to their communities. These figures show that giving back is not just about financial contributions—it's about leveraging resources, time, and influence to address systemic challenges and uplift others.

Philanthropy rooted in authenticity, as seen in these examples, creates lasting legacies far beyond personal achievements. It also serves as a reminder that success can be a platform for service, proving that when individuals prioritize the greater good, their impact extends far beyond their fields of expertise. In doing so, they highlight the profound truth that greatness is not only measured by personal accomplishments but by the lives uplifted along the way.

Conclusion: Create a Life of Vision, Purpose, and Impact

Crafting a compelling vision for your life is a transformative journey that aligns your passions, values, and goals into a roadmap for success and fulfillment. By leveraging tools like visualization, mindfulness, and self-awareness, you can reframe challenges as opportunities and overcome obstacles with resilience. The examples of individuals who turned adversity into triumph—like George Washington Carver, Harland Sanders, and modern philanthropists such as Jon Bon Jovi—underscore the importance of combining personal aspirations with a commitment to service. These stories show how visionaries harness their creativity and determination to shape not only their lives but also the world around them.

A life of vision goes beyond personal achievements; it is enriched by the impact you make on others. Whether through community service, philanthropy, or mentorship, your actions can leave a legacy that inspires and uplifts. Figures like Michael Jordan and Serena Williams demonstrate how leveraging success for the greater good amplifies its meaning, creating ripples of change that benefit countless lives. Their examples remind us that true greatness is not measured solely by what we achieve but by how we contribute to the well-being of others.

When crafting your vision, remember that small steps lead to big transformations. Celebrate incremental wins, reflect on your progress, and remain adaptable in the face of challenges. Harnessing fear as fuel and surrounding yourself with supportive individuals can sustain your momentum and deepen your resolve. Embracing resilience and creativity allows you to shape your beliefs, align them with purposeful action, and unlock a future that excites and drives you.

Key Takeaways

1. **Start with Clarity:** Reflect on your values, passions, and goals to craft a vision that aligns with your authentic self.
2. **Visualize and Act:** Use visualization techniques to create a vivid mental picture of your ideal future and take actionable steps to achieve it.
3. **Reframe Challenges:** See fear and obstacles as opportunities for growth and innovation, not as barriers to success.
4. **Celebrate Progress:** Acknowledge small victories to build confidence and maintain motivation.
5. **Give Back:** Anchor your vision in service and community impact, creating a legacy that inspires others.

6. **Leverage Support:** Surround yourself with uplifting individuals and resources that reinforce your resilience and purpose.
7. **Stay Adaptable:** Regularly revisit and refine your vision to ensure it remains aligned with your evolving aspirations.

By crafting a vision that integrates personal fulfillment and a commitment to greater good, you unlock the power to transform your life and leave a meaningful impact on the world.

"Your vision will become clear only when you can look into your own heart. Who looks outside, dreams; who looks inside, awakes."
– Carl Jung

CHAPTER 7

Mastering Your Mindset: From Fixed to Growth

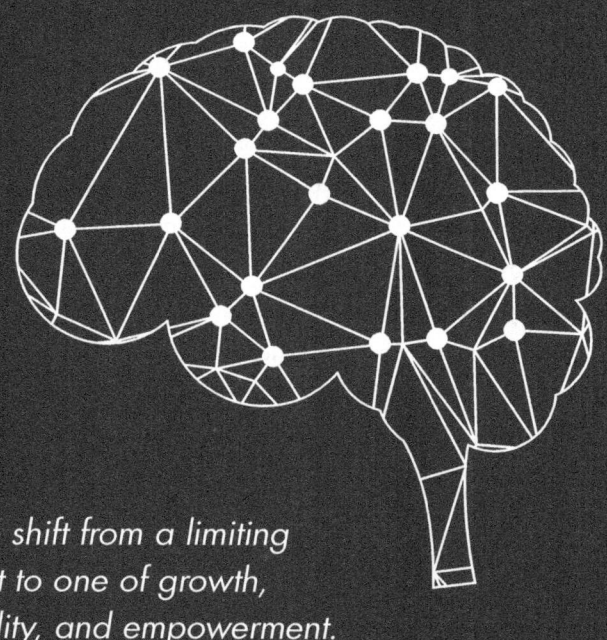

How to shift from a limiting mindset to one of growth, possibility, and empowerment.

Mastering Your Mindset: From Fixed to Growth

The journey from a fixed mindset to a growth mindset begins with understanding the beliefs and attitudes that hold you back. A fixed mindset, as defined by psychologist **Carol Dweck**, assumes that talents and abilities are static, leading individuals to fear failure and avoid challenges. On the other hand, a growth mindset embraces the idea that skills and intelligence can be developed through effort and learning. Shifting to a growth mindset involves reprogramming your thoughts to view challenges as opportunities, failure as feedback, and persistence as a key ingredient for success. It's about embracing the belief that you are capable of growth, even in the face of adversity.

A fascinating example from nature that illustrates a growth-oriented approach is the **bumblebee**. According to traditional aerodynamics, the bumblebee shouldn't be able to fly due to its small wings and large body mass. Yet, it defies these limitations, buzzing along as if unaware of the "impossible" laws of physics. The bumblebee's flight is a metaphor for mastering mindset—when you ignore limiting beliefs and focus on action, you can achieve what others deem improbable. This principle reminds us that sometimes, not knowing what's "impossible" allows us to achieve the extraordinary.

Psychologically, this transformation involves identifying and reframing limiting beliefs. Cognitive-behavioral therapy (CBT) highlights the power of replacing negative thought patterns with empowering ones. For instance, if you think, "I can't succeed at this because I lack talent," you can reframe it to, "I can learn the skills needed to succeed with effort and persistence." Embracing small steps and celebrating progress reinforces this shift. The brain's neuroplasticity ensures that with consistent practice, new thought patterns can replace old ones, enabling a mindset geared toward growth and possibility.

History offers countless examples of individuals who overcame fear and self-imposed limitations to achieve greatness. **Harriet Tubman**: Overcoming Fear to Lead Others to Freedom. Born into slavery in the early 1820s, Harriet Tubman faced a life of severe oppression, physical abuse, and a lack of basic human rights. Despite these circumstances, Tubman refused to accept her imposed limitations. In 1849, fearing she might be sold and separated from her family, Tubman escaped to freedom in the North. However, her story did not end with her own liberation. Over the course of her life, Tubman risked her safety repeatedly to lead approximately 70 enslaved people to freedom via the Underground Railroad.

Tubman's journey required her to confront intense fear—of capture, punishment, and even death. Yet, she channeled this fear into fuel for her mission. Tubman's determination was underpinned by a deep sense of faith and purpose. She often credited her courage to her spiritual beliefs, saying that her visions and guidance from God gave her the strength to persevere. She once famously said, *"I was the conductor of the Underground Railroad for eight years, and I can say what most conductors can't say—I never ran my train off the track, and I never lost a passenger."*

From a psychological perspective, Tubman's resilience can be seen as an example of post-traumatic growth, where adversity becomes a catalyst for profound personal and societal change. Her ability to reframe fear and see it as part of her mission enabled her to push forward. Tubman's unwavering belief in the value of freedom not only shaped her actions but also inspired others to join her cause, despite the risks involved.

Later in life, Tubman reflected on her legacy with humility and pride, knowing that her courage had contributed to the abolition of slavery and the empowerment of generations. Her life reminds us that fear, when faced with purpose and determination, can become a powerful tool for change. Tubman's story continues to inspire countless individuals to overcome limitations and fight for justice, proving that courage is not the absence of fear but the triumph over it.

Mastering your mindset means shifting from limitations to empowerment by challenging assumptions, embracing challenges, and celebrating progress. The bumblebee flies despite its supposed aerodynamic limitations, and individuals like Harriet Tubman overcome fear and adversity to reshape history. By adopting a growth mindset, you open the door to new possibilities, empowering yourself to achieve success beyond what you once believed was possible.

Reshaping beliefs and transforming from a mindset of limitations to one of limitless possibilities involves a combination of self-awareness, intentional effort, and practical strategies. Below are key steps to help reframe limiting beliefs and cultivate empowering ones:

1. Identify and Challenge Limiting Beliefs

- What to Do: Begin by recognizing the specific beliefs that hold you back. Ask yourself:
  - What recurring negative thoughts do I have about my abilities or potential?
  - Are these beliefs rooted in facts or assumptions?
- Psychological Insight: Use cognitive restructuring, a technique from Cognitive Behavioral Therapy (CBT), to challenge and replace distorted beliefs. For example, if you believe, "I'll never succeed," counter it with evidence of past successes or efforts that have led to growth.
- Practical Exercise: Write down your limiting beliefs and then create an opposing, empowering belief. Repeat the empowering belief daily as an affirmation.

2. Adopt a Growth Mindset

- What to Do: Shift your perspective to see challenges as opportunities for growth rather than threats. Focus on learning from failures and celebrating progress.
- Embracing a growth mindset emphasizes the idea that abilities can be developed through dedication and effort. Embracing this mindset fosters resilience and a willingness to take on new challenges.
- Practical Exercise: When faced with setbacks, ask yourself:
  - What can I learn from this?
  - How can I improve next time?
- Emphasize the process rather than the outcome, reinforcing the idea that progress is possible.

3. Reframe Negative Thoughts

- What to Do: Train your mind to interpret challenges and fears in a more constructive way.
- Psychological Insight: Reframing involves shifting your interpretation of a situation to focus on its positive or neutral aspects. For instance, instead of saying, "This is too hard," reframe it as, "This is an opportunity to grow stronger."
- Practical Exercise: Use a journal to write down negative thoughts and then rewrite them with a positive spin. For example:
  - ☼ Negative Thought: "I'm not good at public speaking."
  - ☼ Reframed Thought: "I'm learning to improve my public speaking skills with practice."

4. Use Visualization and Affirmations

- What to Do: Visualize yourself achieving your goals and living your best life. Combine this with affirmations that reinforce your new beliefs.
- Psychological Insight: Visualization activates neural pathways associated with success, making goals feel more attainable. Affirmations, when repeated consistently, help rewire the subconscious mind.
- Practical Exercise: Spend 5-10 minutes daily visualizing your ideal self and repeat affirmations like:
  - ☼ "I am capable of achieving anything I set my mind to."
  - ☼ "I attract opportunities that align with my highest potential."

5. Surround Yourself with Positive Influences

- What to Do: Engage with people, resources, and environments that support your growth and encourage limitless thinking.
- Psychological Insight: The social learning theory suggests that behaviors and attitudes are influenced by observing and interacting

with others. Surrounding yourself with positive role models reinforces empowering beliefs.
- Practical Exercise: Join communities, read books, or listen to podcasts that inspire growth. Limit exposure to negativity or criticism that reinforces limiting beliefs.

6. Take Action and Build Momentum

- What to Do: Start small, and take consistent steps toward your goals. Each success reinforces your new beliefs.
- Psychological Insight: Behavioral activation emphasizes that action leads to emotional and mental shifts. As you take steps, your brain rewires itself to associate effort with positive outcomes.
- Practical Exercise: Set one small, achievable goal each week that aligns with your vision. Celebrate each accomplishment, no matter how minor.

7. Practice Self-Compassion

- What to Do: Be kind to yourself as you navigate this journey. Understand that change takes time and setbacks are part of the process.
- Psychological Insight: Self-compassion reduces fear of failure and encourages persistence. According to Dr. Kristin Neff, it involves treating yourself with the same kindness you would offer a friend.
- Practical Exercise: When you make a mistake, remind yourself:
  - ☼ "Everyone makes mistakes. This is an opportunity to learn and grow."

8. Anchor New Beliefs with Evidence

- What to Do: Collect evidence of your progress and success to reinforce your new beliefs.

- Psychological Insight: The brain tends to focus on what it is trained to notice (confirmation bias). By actively seeking proof of your abilities, you solidify empowering beliefs.
- Practical Exercise: Maintain a "Success Journal" where you record daily wins, breakthroughs, and moments of courage. Review it regularly to remind yourself of your progress.

Conclusion: Empowering Transformation Through Mindset Mastery

Mastering your mindset is a transformative journey that begins with self-awareness and intentional effort to replace limiting beliefs with empowering ones. By embracing a growth mindset, reframing challenges as opportunities, and practicing self-compassion, you can unlock your potential and achieve success beyond what you once thought possible. Like the bumblebee, which defies aerodynamic limitations to soar, individuals who shed fixed thinking can achieve remarkable feats by focusing on possibilities rather than constraints. This journey not only enhances personal growth but also fosters resilience, enabling you to navigate life's challenges with confidence and adaptability.

A key to this transformation is using practical tools such as visualization, affirmations, and cognitive reframing to reprogram the subconscious mind. These techniques leverage neuroplasticity, allowing the brain to form new, empowering thought patterns that align with your goals. Surrounding yourself with positive influences—people, communities, and resources—further reinforces your ability to maintain a limitless mindset. By taking small, consistent actions and celebrating incremental successes, you build momentum and solidify your belief in your capacity to grow and succeed.

History offers countless examples of individuals who reshaped their lives through mindset mastery, such as Harriet Tubman, whose unyielding determination and courage overcame fear and adversity to change history. Modern practices like maintaining a success journal and using affirmations to anchor new beliefs provide actionable ways to follow in the footsteps of such visionaries. These strategies remind us that setbacks and failures are not endpoints but stepping stones to greatness.

Ultimately, reshaping your beliefs and adopting a limitless mindset empowers you to create a life of purpose and fulfillment. By aligning your thoughts, emotions, and actions with your aspirations, you can achieve extraordinary growth and make a meaningful impact on the world. Now is the time to take bold steps, challenge assumptions, and craft a life that excites and drives you.

Key Takeaway Points

1. **Identify and Challenge Limiting Beliefs**: Recognize self-imposed barriers and replace them with empowering beliefs through tools like cognitive restructuring.
2. **Embrace a Growth Mindset**: View challenges as opportunities for growth and learn from failures to foster resilience.
3. **Reframe Negative Thoughts**: Shift perspectives to focus on possibilities and strengths rather than obstacles.
4. **Visualize and Affirm Success**: Use visualization and affirmations to create mental blueprints for achieving your goals.
5. **Surround Yourself with Positivity**: Build a support network of inspiring individuals and resources that encourage growth.
6. **Take Action and Celebrate Progress**: Start small and celebrate every achievement to build momentum and confidence.
7. **Practice Self-Compassion**: Treat yourself with kindness and understanding, especially during setbacks.
8. **Anchor New Beliefs with Evidence**: Keep a success journal to reinforce positive progress and solidify a limitless mindset.

Shifting from a fixed mindset to a growth-oriented one is a transformative journey that opens doors to new possibilities and empowerment. By challenging limiting beliefs, embracing learning opportunities, visualizing success, and surrounding yourself with positive influences, you can reprogram your mind for growth and resilience. Remember, mastery of your mindset is not an overnight process—it's a practice that evolves with every step you take toward your goals. Empower yourself to view challenges as stepping stones, and you'll unlock a world of potential waiting within.

"The greatest achievements arise not from the certainty of possibility, but from the courage to act when others see only impossibility."

CHAPTER 8

Limitless Growth: How Challenges Shape Extraordinary Futures

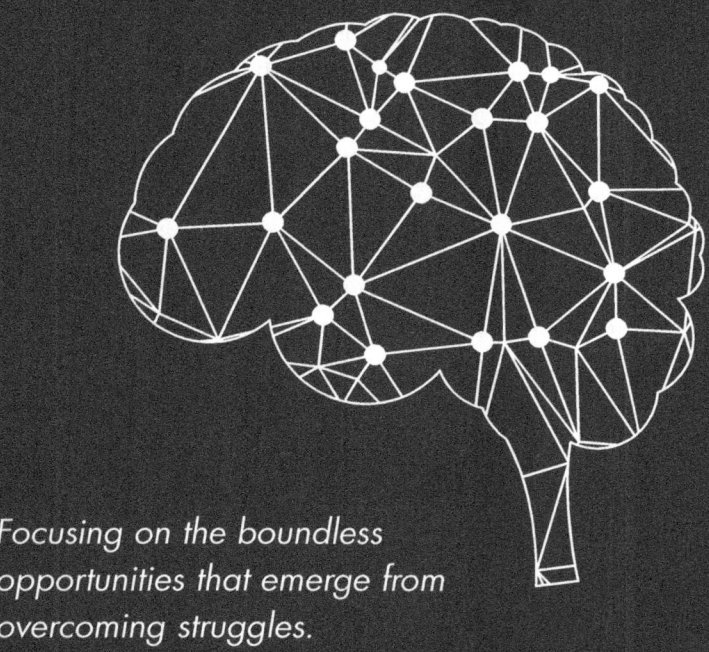

Focusing on the boundless opportunities that emerge from overcoming struggles.

The concept of *Limitless Growth: How Challenges Shape Extraordinary Futures* highlights the transformative power of adversity. While challenges can be uncomfortable or painful, they often serve as catalysts for profound growth, transformation, and success. Drawing insights from psychology, history, sports, space exploration, and nature, this perspective offers a multidisciplinary understanding of how overcoming struggles unlocks boundless opportunities for advancement.

Throughout history, humanity's progress has hinged on the willingness of individuals to face the unknown and embrace the risks that come with it. In the earliest days of human civilization, survival itself was a process of trial and error. Consider the discovery of edible plants or new food sources—someone had to be the first to taste an unfamiliar fruit, root, or herb, often at great personal risk. Tragically, some perished from consuming poisonous substances, yet their sacrifices provided critical knowledge that saved others and expanded humanity's understanding of the natural world. These early pioneers laid the foundation for the collective growth of their communities, turning uncertainty into survival strategies that propelled human advancement.

This same spirit of trailblazing extends into modern science and medicine. Volunteers for clinical trials, often referred to as "guinea pigs," knowingly expose themselves to potential risks to test new treatments and drugs that might benefit humanity as a whole. For example, in the mid-20th century, volunteers risked their lives during the development of vaccines for deadly diseases like polio. Their courage and willingness to face uncertainty paved the way for breakthroughs that saved millions of lives. These acts of bravery underscore how progress often comes at the cost of individual hardship, but the ripple effects create opportunities for extraordinary growth and advancement.

This pattern of facing challenges, enduring risks, and transforming struggles into knowledge underscores a profound truth: growth is rarely without sacrifice. Whether in the ancient world of foraging or the modern laboratories of medical science, overcoming obstacles has been humanity's ticket to resilience and innovation. These stories remind us that growth is a collective legacy, carried forward by those who dare to step into the unknown and shape a brighter, limitless future for all.

Key Themes in Limitless Growth

1. Challenges as Growth Catalysts

In psychology, the concept of **post-traumatic growth (PTG)** illustrates how adversity, while painful, can serve as a powerful catalyst for transformation and self-discovery. PTG refers to the positive psychological change experienced as a result of struggling with challenging circumstances. Unlike mere resilience, which helps individuals return to their baseline state, PTG enables them to surpass their previous levels of functioning, developing new strengths, perspectives, and life priorities. Research in this field highlights how enduring hardships can foster profound personal growth, allowing individuals to tap into reservoirs of potential they never knew existed.

Struggling through adversity often unlocks new perspectives on life and its possibilities. People who face significant challenges, such as recovering from a debilitating illness or navigating a personal loss, frequently report a greater appreciation for life's simple joys and a deeper connection to their values. For instance, a person recovering from a career setback may initially feel defeated, but the experience can serve as a wake-up call, prompting them to reevaluate their goals and discover entrepreneurial grit or creative potential they hadn't explored. This reframing of challenges into opportunities aligns with the growth mindset, where obstacles are seen as stepping stones rather than roadblocks.

A striking example of PTG comes from the world of medicine, where doctors and researchers have turned personal adversity into groundbreaking contributions. Consider **Dr. Viktor Frankl**, a Holocaust survivor and renowned psychiatrist, who endured unimaginable suffering in concentration camps during World War II. Rather than succumbing to despair, he emerged with a profound understanding of the human capacity for meaning-making. His experiences became the foundation for his groundbreaking work, **"Man's Search for Meaning,"** which continues to inspire countless individuals to find purpose even in life's darkest moments.

These stories underscore the transformative power of challenges. Struggles may feel overwhelming in the moment, but they often reveal strengths, passions, and possibilities that remain hidden in times of ease. By embracing challenges as opportunities for growth, individuals not only overcome adversity but also discover new dimensions of themselves and their potential. This shift in perspective is not just life-changing—it is life-expanding, paving the way for extraordinary futures built on the foundation of perseverance and self-discovery.

2. Learning Through Failure

Some individuals derive greater value from their failures than others because they actively analyze and incorporate the lessons learned into their subsequent efforts. Rather than merely moving past setbacks, these people approach failure as a critical learning opportunity, dissecting what went wrong, identifying overlooked factors, and adapting their strategies accordingly. This process not only builds resilience but also enhances their capacity to innovate and succeed in the long term.

Psychologically, this mindset aligns with the concept of a **growth mindset**, as introduced by psychologist **Carol Dweck**. Those with a growth mindset view failures as opportunities for improvement rather than as fixed indictments of their abilities. They engage in reflective practices, seeking feedback and challenging their assumptions, which helps them refine their approach and make more informed decisions moving forward.

For example, a scientist working on a complex experiment might experience repeated failures before achieving a breakthrough. Instead of abandoning the project, they meticulously analyze each failed attempt, tweaking variables and refining methods. This iterative learning process is evident in the journey of **Thomas Edison**, who famously said, *"I have not failed. I've just found 10,000 ways that won't work."* By systematically learning from each misstep, **Edison** eventually succeeded in creating the light bulb, revolutionizing modern life.

Ultimately, the ability to extract meaningful lessons from failure and apply them strategically is what separates those who stagnate from those who achieve extraordinary success. By embracing failure as a necessary step in the learning process, individuals develop the adaptability and perseverance required to turn setbacks into building blocks for growth.

The process of failing and rising again is integral to achieving extraordinary futures. Failure teaches lessons, builds resilience, and fosters a mindset that values progress over perfection. **As Stephen Hawking** once said, "However difficult life may seem, there is always something you can do and succeed at." Despite living with ALS, which severely limited his physical abilities, Hawking transformed his challenges into opportunities for groundbreaking scientific contributions. His work in theoretical physics, particularly on black holes, stands as a testament to the power of perseverance and resilience in the face of unimaginable difficulty.

3. Sports as a Metaphor

Sports provide some of the most inspiring examples of turning challenges into triumphs, showcasing the human spirit's capacity to rise above adversity. Athletes who confront physical, mental, and competitive barriers often use these challenges as catalysts for growth, resilience, and eventual greatness. One such example is Sammy Lee, a trailblazing diver and the first Asian-American to win an Olympic gold medal for the United States. His journey is a testament to the power of determination, creativity, and unwavering resolve in the face of immense obstacles.

Sammy Lee faced significant racial discrimination and limited access to proper training facilities as a young athlete in the 1930s and 1940s. In Pasadena, California, where he trained, public swimming pools were only open to people of color one day a week—on what was disparagingly called "International Day," after which the pools were drained and cleaned. Undeterred, Lee found innovative ways to hone his skills. He practiced his dives in makeshift sand pits in his backyard, using the unforgiving surface to perfect his form and landings. This unorthodox training method not only demonstrated his resourcefulness but also refined his technique, giving him an edge over competitors who trained in more conventional settings.

Lee's resilience and dedication paid off in extraordinary ways. At the 1948 London Olympics, he won gold in the 10-meter platform diving event, breaking barriers for Asian-Americans in sports. Four years later, he defended his title with another gold medal at the 1952 Helsinki Olympics, solidifying his legacy as one of the greatest divers of his era. Beyond his athletic accomplishments, Lee pursued a medical degree and became a renowned physician, proving that his drive for excellence extended far beyond the diving board.

Sammy Lee's story serves as a powerful reminder that challenges often fuel greatness when paired with resilience, ingenuity, and a refusal to accept limitations. His ability to transform adversity into opportunity not only paved the way for future generations of Asian-American athletes but also stands as a universal example of how creativity and perseverance can overcome systemic barriers. By defying the odds, Lee left a legacy of excellence and empowerment, inspiring countless others to pursue their dreams, regardless of the obstacles in their path.

4. Space Exploration: A Testament to Human Resilience

Space exploration epitomizes humanity's ability to overcome the seemingly impossible, pushing the boundaries of what is achievable. One of the most compelling examples of this resilience is NASA's Apollo 13 mission, which turned potential catastrophe into a story of remarkable ingenuity and teamwork. In 1970, the mission was intended to be the third lunar landing. However, just two days into the journey, an oxygen tank exploded, crippling the spacecraft and jeopardizing the lives of the three astronauts on board—Jim Lovell, Jack Swigert, and Fred Haise. The explosion rendered the mission to the moon impossible, forcing the crew and mission control to focus entirely on survival and safe return to Earth.

Faced with dwindling resources, freezing temperatures, and rising carbon dioxide levels, both the astronauts and NASA's mission control had to adapt rapidly. Engineers on the ground worked around the clock, simulating solutions with limited tools and materials available aboard the spacecraft. Their ingenuity led to the development of a makeshift air filtration system using items as rudimentary as duct tape, a plastic bag, and a sock. This resourcefulness demonstrated the extraordinary capacity of the human mind to innovate under pressure, transforming what seemed like an insurmountable obstacle into a workable solution.

Equally critical was the astronauts' mental resilience. Operating in the confined and precarious environment of the lunar module, which was repurposed as a lifeboat, the crew remained focused, coordinated, and disciplined. Jim Lovell's leadership played a pivotal role in maintaining morale and ensuring clear communication between the spacecraft and mission control. Despite the physical and psychological strain, the team relied on their training, creativity, and unwavering determination to navigate the crisis. Their ability to adapt showcased how resilience and teamwork are vital components of overcoming challenges.

Apollo 13's successful return to Earth was hailed as a "successful failure," demonstrating that extraordinary growth and innovation often emerge from adversity. This mission highlighted humanity's capacity to thrive under the most extreme circumstances, proving that the impossible can be achieved when challenges are met with perseverance and collaboration. The legacy of Apollo 13 serves as an enduring reminder that even in the direst situations, the human spirit is capable of overcoming seemingly insurmountable odds and reaching for the stars.

5. Historical and Frontier Perspectives

The old west and stories of pioneers embody the concept of overcoming adversity to create extraordinary futures. Settlers faced treacherous terrain, scarce resources, and constant uncertainty. Yet, their resilience paved the way for growth and innovation, from establishing communities to expanding industries. Figures like **Sacagawea**, who guided the **Lewis and Clark expedition**, underscore how adaptability and courage can reshape futures.

6. Mindset and Beliefs

Adopting a **growth mindset**—the belief that abilities can be developed through effort, learning, and persistence—is crucial for limitless growth. **Neuroplasticity**, the brain's ability to adapt and form new neural connections, reinforces that even deeply ingrained habits or beliefs can be reshaped. Visualization, affirmations, and other tools from **Neuro-Linguistic Programming (NLP)** can help individuals rewire their minds for success, reinforcing the belief that challenges are stepping stones rather than roadblocks.

Conclusion: Limitless Growth—How Challenges Shape Extraordinary Futures

The concept of **limitless growth** emphasizes the transformative power of challenges and adversity. Obstacles are not merely roadblocks; they are opportunities for profound growth, innovation, and discovery. Throughout history, from the pioneers of the Old West to modern astronauts and trailblazing athletes, extraordinary individuals have demonstrated that challenges often serve as the catalysts for greatness. By facing these obstacles with resilience, creativity, and an open mindset, they have reshaped their futures and left indelible legacies.

Adversity sparks growth by encouraging resourcefulness, adaptability, and grit. Whether it's Sammy Lee refining his diving technique in sand pits due to racial discrimination or the Apollo 13 team engineering life-saving solutions in the depths of space, these stories illustrate humanity's capacity to turn limitations into triumphs. In every instance, a common thread emerges: the refusal to surrender to circumstances. Instead, these individuals chose to meet their struggles head-on, transforming personal hardships into stepping stones for progress.

In psychology, the concept of **post-traumatic growth** (PTG) validates this transformative process, showing how adversity can lead to heightened resilience, newfound perspectives, and greater personal strength. Similarly, the **growth mindset** reinforces the idea that abilities can be cultivated through effort and learning, turning failures into opportunities for improvement. These mental frameworks encourage us to embrace challenges rather than shy away from them, reinforcing that growth often lies on the other side of discomfort.

From Sacagawea navigating uncharted terrain to Stephen Hawking transcending the physical limitations of ALS to revolutionize physics, history is filled with examples of individuals who overcame extraordinary challenges. They remind us that our mindset, determination, and actions define how we respond to adversity. Tools like **visualization**, **affirmations**, and **neuro-linguistic programming** (NLP) further underscore the potential to reprogram beliefs and turn obstacles into opportunities.

Key Points

1. **Adversity Fuels Growth**: Challenges are opportunities to build resilience, innovate, and discover untapped potential.
2. **Mindset Matters**: Adopting a growth mindset transforms failures into lessons and strengthens perseverance.
3. **History Teaches Us**: Figures like Sammy Lee, Sacagawea, and Stephen Hawking exemplify how extraordinary futures emerge from overcoming struggles.
4. **Psychological Tools for Success**: Techniques such as visualization and NLP empower individuals to reframe limitations and harness opportunities.
5. **The Ripple Effect of Growth**: Individual breakthroughs inspire collective progress, demonstrating how personal triumphs contribute to the greater good.

By embracing a mindset of limitless growth, we can view challenges not as setbacks but as springboards for extraordinary futures. With determination, creativity, and the belief that no obstacle is insurmountable, we unlock the potential to transform our lives and make a lasting impact on the world.

Practical Steps to Cultivate Limitless Growth

1. **Reframe Challenges**: View obstacles as opportunities for learning and personal development.
2. **Set Incremental Goals**: Break larger challenges into smaller, actionable steps to build confidence and momentum.
3. **Cultivate Resilience**: Practice mindfulness, gratitude, and self-compassion to navigate setbacks with grace.
4. **Seek Inspiration**: Draw from stories of historical figures, athletes, and pioneers who turned adversity into triumph.
5. **Reflect and Adjust**: Regularly assess what challenges have taught you and adapt your strategies accordingly.

Why This Concept Matters

By embracing challenges as essential to growth, individuals can unlock potential they didn't realize they possessed. This philosophy fosters innovation, creativity, and resilience, empowering people to move beyond their perceived limitations. It demonstrates that through persistence, adaptability, and the right mindset, extraordinary futures are not just possible—they are inevitable.

> *"A gem cannot be polished without friction,*
> *nor a man perfected without trials."*
> — Chinese Proverb

This timeless saying emphasizes that challenges and hardships are necessary for growth and refinement, much like friction is needed to bring out the brilliance of a gemstone. It suggests that struggles are not merely obstacles but essential parts of the journey toward excellence and success.

CHAPTER 9

The Art of Self-Compassion and Accountability

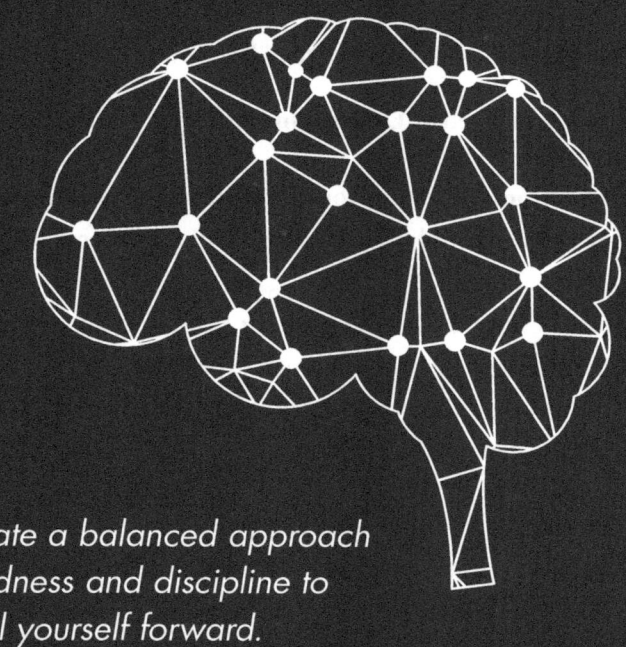

Cultivate a balanced approach of kindness and discipline to propel yourself forward.

The Art of Self-Compassion and Accountability is a transformative concept that weaves together kindness toward oneself with a commitment to personal responsibility and growth. Self-compassion, as defined by psychologist Dr. Kristin Neff, involves treating yourself with the same understanding and care that you would offer to a close friend. This practice helps mitigate the harmful effects of self-criticism, which can lead to feelings of inadequacy and hinder progress. Accountability, on the other hand, involves taking ownership of your actions, decisions, and outcomes, ensuring that you remain focused on your goals and committed to self-improvement. Together, these two principles create a harmonious balance that allows individuals to face challenges with resilience and purpose while maintaining their mental and emotional well-being.

Self-Compassion: A Foundation for Growth

Self-compassion, as defined by **Dr. Kristin Neff**, involves three components:

1. **Self-Kindness:** Treating yourself with the same care and understanding you would offer a friend during moments of failure or difficulty.
2. **Common Humanity:** Recognizing that struggles and imperfections are part of the shared human experience.
3. **Mindfulness:** Observing your emotions and thoughts without judgment or over-identification.

Self-compassion enables individuals to approach setbacks with empathy rather than harsh self-criticism, which is often counterproductive. Research has shown that people who practice self-compassion are more likely to recover from failures and maintain motivation, as they are less likely to be paralyzed by shame or guilt.

How to treat yourself with Self-Kindness

Treating yourself with care and understanding involves cultivating self-compassion and prioritizing your emotional, physical, and mental well-being. Below are practical ways to practice self-care and show kindness to yourself:

1. Practice Positive Self-Talk

- Replace self-critical thoughts with compassionate and encouraging language.
- For example, instead of saying, "I can't believe I messed up," say, "Everyone makes mistakes; this is an opportunity to learn."
- Affirmations like, "I am doing my best," or "I deserve kindness and patience," can help reinforce self-worth.

2. Set Healthy Boundaries

- Learn to say no to obligations or relationships that drain your energy or compromise your well-being.
- Protect your time and prioritize activities that align with your values and bring you joy.
- Boundaries are a form of self-respect and self-preservation.

3. Acknowledge Your Emotions

- Allow yourself to feel and process emotions without judgment.
- Journaling can be a powerful tool to explore your feelings and understand what you need in the moment.
- Remind yourself that it's okay to feel vulnerable or overwhelmed; these emotions are part of being human.

4. Engage in Mindfulness Practices

- Spend a few minutes each day focusing on the present moment through meditation, deep breathing, or yoga.
- Mindfulness reduces stress and enhances self-awareness, helping you respond to challenges with calmness and clarity.

5. Celebrate Your Wins

- Acknowledge your accomplishments, no matter how small.
- Keep a journal or a "success jar" where you note moments of progress, gratitude, or pride.
- Celebrating yourself reinforces positive self-regard.

6. Prioritize Rest and Relaxation

- Ensure you get adequate sleep and take breaks during the day to recharge.
- Incorporate activities that relax you, such as reading, taking a bath, or enjoying nature.

7. Take Care of Your Physical Health

- Nourish your body with balanced meals, regular exercise, and hydration.
- Treat your body as you would a trusted friend, offering it care and attention.

8. Seek Support

- Reach out to friends, family, or a therapist for encouragement or to share your feelings.
- Surround yourself with people who uplift and understand you.

9. Forgive Yourself

- Let go of past mistakes or regrets by practicing self-forgiveness.
- Remind yourself that everyone makes mistakes, and growth comes from learning and moving forward.

10. Engage in Activities You Love

- Make time for hobbies or activities that bring you joy and fulfillment.
- Whether it's painting, cooking, or playing a sport, doing things you love reminds you of your intrinsic value.

11. Focus on Gratitude

- Regularly reflect on what you're grateful for, including qualities you appreciate about yourself.
- Gratitude shifts focus from what's lacking to what's abundant in your life.

By adopting these practices, you nurture a supportive relationship with yourself, building resilience and creating a foundation for a fulfilling and balanced life.

Accountability: Taking Ownership of Growth

Accountability involves taking responsibility for your actions, decisions, and their outcomes. It's the practice of holding yourself to the commitments and standards you've set. Accountability fosters discipline and ensures that self-compassion does not become an excuse for complacency. When paired with self-compassion, accountability becomes a powerful tool for self-improvement without the weight of self-judgment.

Psychological research highlights the importance of "self-determination theory," which posits that individuals thrive when they feel in control of their actions and outcomes. By taking accountability, individuals reinforce their sense of agency and ownership, which strengthens intrinsic motivation and fosters growth.

The Balance Between Self-Compassion and Accountability

Balancing these two concepts involves understanding that self-compassion provides the emotional safety to acknowledge mistakes, while accountability drives the resolve to learn and improve. For example:

- Without self-compassion, accountability can lead to burnout and self-doubt.
- Without accountability, self-compassion can lead to stagnation and avoidance of growth.

Yin (Self-Compassion) and Yang (Accountability) vs Self-Compassion and Accountability

The concepts of **Self-Compassion** and **Accountability** are very much aligned with the yin and yang philosophy. In Chinese philosophy, **yin and yang** represent complementary forces that, while seemingly opposite, are interconnected and interdependent. Together, they create harmony and balance. Similarly, **self-compassion and accountability** balance each other, ensuring growth and well-being without tipping into extremes.

Here's how the **yin and yang** dynamic maps onto these two principles:

Yin (Self-Compassion)

- Represents softness, nurturing, and emotional safety.
- Provides the foundation for self-acceptance, healing, and emotional resilience.

- Encourages forgiveness, understanding, and a focus on intrinsic worth, helping individuals recover from setbacks and maintain mental well-being.

Without the "yin" of self-compassion:

- Accountability may become overly harsh, leading to burnout, perfectionism, or self-criticism.
- Individuals may fear failure, which can stifle creativity and risk-taking.

Yang (Accountability)

- Represents structure, action, and forward momentum.
- Drives the determination to take responsibility, set goals, and work toward improvement.
- Ensures that self-compassion doesn't slip into complacency or avoidance.

Without the "yang" of accountability:

- Self-compassion may lead to stagnation, enabling excuses rather than fostering growth.
- Individuals might fail to address areas where change or effort is needed for personal development.

The Harmony Between the Two

When self-compassion (yin) and accountability (yang) are balanced:

- **Growth Flourishes**: Self-compassion allows individuals to face mistakes without fear, while accountability ensures they take proactive steps to learn and grow.
- **Emotional Resilience Develops**: Compassion fosters self-worth, and accountability builds competence and confidence.

- **Long-Term Success**: The combination ensures sustainable progress without sacrificing mental and emotional well-being.

Example in Action

A student who performs poorly on an exam can balance self-compassion and accountability:

- **Self-Compassion (Yin)**: "It's okay to feel disappointed. I'm human, and this doesn't define my worth."
- **Accountability (Yang)**: "What can I do differently next time? I'll seek help, adjust my study methods, and dedicate more time to preparation."

Together, these forces create a mindset that nurtures emotional health while driving meaningful growth, embodying the harmony central to the yin and yang philosophy.

Consider a well-known example from Chinese history that illustrates the **yin and yang principle** is the story of **Qin Shi Huang**, the first Emperor of China. While his life and actions reflect a deep desire for balance and unity, his obsession with immortality and life extension led to his downfall—highlighting the consequences of an imbalance between opposing forces.

The Context

Qin Shi Huang, who unified China in 221 BCE, is a figure both admired and criticized. His achievements, such as standardizing the written script, currency, and measurements, reflect his ability to harmonize disparate elements into a cohesive whole, embodying the **yang** of action, ambition, and progress. However, his unrelenting drive to conquer not just his enemies but also death itself tipped the balance, leading to destructive consequences.

The Obsession with Immortality

Obsessed with extending his life, Qin Shi Huang sought elixirs that he believed would grant him eternal life. His court alchemists and advisers, operating under the principle of seeking balance between life and death (yin and yang), proposed remedies that often-contained toxic substances, including mercury. Mercury was thought to embody the yin element of water and was mistakenly believed to have life-preserving qualities. Ironically, instead of achieving immortality, his ingestion of mercury caused severe health problems, including physical deterioration, madness, and ultimately his death in 210 BCE.

The Yin and Yang Lesson

Qin Shi Huang's story illustrates what happens when the **yang** force (action and ambition) overpowers **yin** (restraint and acceptance of natural limits). His desire to control and extend life disrupted the natural balance, leading to unintended consequences.

Broader Implications

This historical example serves as a cautionary tale about the dangers of imbalance:

- **Excessive Yang**: Overreach, such as Qin Shi Huang's relentless pursuit of life extension, can lead to self-destruction.
- **Insufficient Yin**: A lack of acceptance of natural limits and cycles (life and death) can prevent harmony and result in unintended harm.

Modern Reflection

The yin and yang principle teaches us that true harmony comes from balancing action and ambition with introspection and acceptance. Qin Shi Huang's life offers a lesson on the importance of humility and respecting the natural order, even in the face of great power and ambition. This historical narrative continues to resonate as a reminder of how imbalance—whether in leadership, health, or personal goals—can lead to dire consequences.

Real-Life Example: Tiger Woods

Tiger Woods provides a compelling example of self-compassion and accountability in action. After dominating the world of professional golf, Woods faced significant personal and professional challenges, including injuries and highly publicized personal struggles. Instead of succumbing to self-pity or giving up, Woods took ownership of his setbacks. He openly acknowledged his mistakes, committed to personal growth, and worked tirelessly to rehabilitate both his health and his game.

Through self-compassion, Woods allowed himself to process his challenges without being defined by them. At the same time, his accountability pushed him to rebuild his skills and mental resilience. His comeback victory at the 2019 Masters—a tournament many thought he would never win again—stands as a testament to his ability to balance kindness to himself with relentless discipline and focus. Woods's journey reminds us that extraordinary achievements often arise from the interplay of personal reflection, responsibility, and resilience.

Practical Applications

To practice the art of self-compassion and accountability:

1. **Adopt a Growth Mindset:** See failures as opportunities for learning rather than as fixed indicators of your worth.

2. **Set Realistic Goals:** Hold yourself accountable for progress while being kind when circumstances don't align perfectly.
3. **Reflect Regularly:** Use journaling to explore what went well, what could improve, and how you'll move forward constructively.
4. **Celebrate Progress:** Acknowledge your achievements, however small, to maintain motivation and self-esteem.

Conclusion: Embracing the Art of Self-Compassion and Accountability

The Art of Self-Compassion and Accountability represents a dynamic balance between kindness to oneself and a steadfast commitment to personal growth. By integrating self-compassion, individuals create a safe emotional space to acknowledge and process challenges without succumbing to self-criticism. Simultaneously, accountability fosters action and responsibility, ensuring progress toward meaningful goals. Together, these principles nurture resilience, enhance well-being, and drive sustainable success.

Through historical and modern examples, such as the yin and yang philosophy, Qin Shi Huang's cautionary tale, and Tiger Woods's triumphant journey, we see the power of harmony between acceptance and ambition. Qin Shi Huang's imbalance highlights the dangers of overreach and neglecting natural limits, while Woods's comeback illustrates how reflection, ownership, and determination can lead to transformative growth. These narratives demonstrate that while self-compassion provides emotional strength, accountability fuels purposeful action—two forces that together enable extraordinary achievements.

Practicing this balance in daily life involves cultivating mindfulness, setting realistic goals, and viewing challenges as opportunities for learning. Practical strategies such as reframing failures, celebrating small wins, and seeking support create an environment where both self-compassion and accountability can thrive. This dual approach ensures that individuals not only navigate setbacks with grace but also continually strive for excellence without compromising their mental and emotional health.

As you embark on your journey of self-improvement, remember that the key to limitless growth lies in embracing both your vulnerabilities and your potential. By treating yourself with care and understanding while holding yourself accountable for progress, you unlock the ability to face challenges with courage, adapt with resilience, and achieve success that is both meaningful and sustainable. This delicate interplay of compassion and responsibility transforms struggles into stepping stones and aspirations into reality, creating a life of fulfillment and boundless possibilities.

To harmonize the forces within, one must embrace the dual truths: to nurture oneself with kindness and to guide oneself with purpose. In softness lies strength, and in action, there is wisdom.
— *Unknown*

CHAPTER 10

Living Authentically: Aligning Your Actions with Your Values

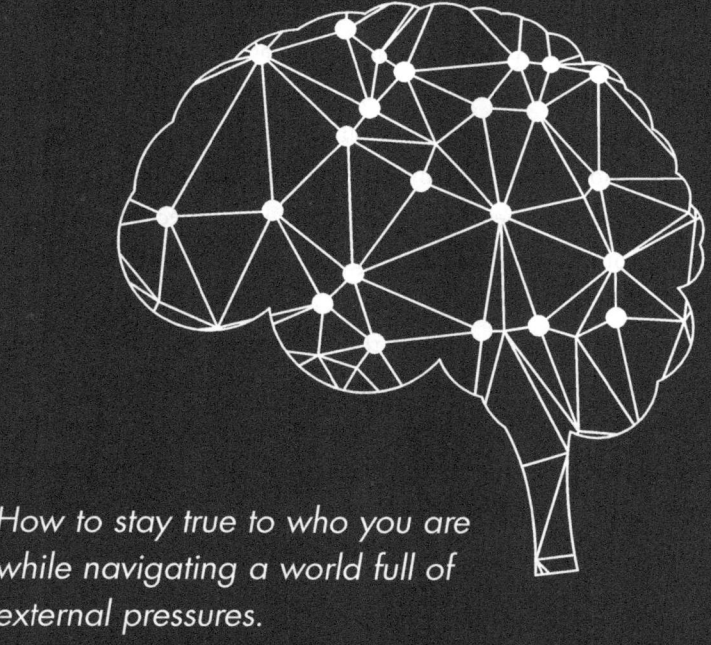

How to stay true to who you are while navigating a world full of external pressures.

Living Authentically: Aligning Your Actions with Your Values

Living authentically means aligning your actions with your core values and beliefs, allowing your behavior to reflect your true self. This involves a deep understanding of who you are and what truly matters to you. Authentic living requires courage—the courage to embrace vulnerability, to make choices that may go against societal expectations, and to remain steadfast in your principles, even in the face of external pressures. By living in alignment with your inner truths, you cultivate a life of integrity, resilience, and purpose, where your actions and decisions are driven by what you genuinely believe and desire.

To live authentically, you must first develop self-awareness. This involves reflecting on your values, beliefs, and passions, and recognizing the influences that may pull you away from them. Self-awareness helps you identify when you are acting out of obligation, fear, or a desire to please others, rather than staying true to yourself. Self-acceptance follows as an essential element, allowing you to embrace your imperfections and celebrate your unique qualities. Authenticity does not mean perfection; rather, it means honoring your humanity, including your strengths and vulnerabilities, as part of your genuine self.

Living authentically also requires the willingness to make difficult choices. Often, being true to yourself means standing out or saying "no" to things that do not align with your values. It might involve pursuing a career that fulfills your passions but diverges from traditional expectations or taking a stand for something you believe in, even when it's unpopular. When you express your genuine self in thoughts, words, and actions, you foster deeper and more meaningful connections with others. People are naturally drawn to authenticity because it conveys trustworthiness, openness, and sincerity.

The rewards of authentic living are profound. It creates a foundation of self-respect and inner peace, allowing you to navigate life with greater confidence and clarity. It fosters resilience, as you are anchored in your own truths rather than swayed by external validation. Moreover, authenticity inspires others, empowering them to live more fully and embrace their own uniqueness. In this way, living authentically is not just a gift to yourself—it is a way of enriching the world around you, one genuine act at a time.

Core Principles of Living Authentically

1. **Self-Awareness:**
   - Living authentically begins with understanding your values, priorities, and passions. By knowing what truly matters, you can assess whether your actions align with these principles.
   - Practices like mindfulness, journaling, and introspection can help uncover the beliefs that define you.

2. **Vulnerability and Connection:**
   - Authenticity requires the courage to express your true thoughts and emotions, even when doing so feels uncomfortable. Vulnerability fosters genuine connections with others, strengthening relationships and building trust.

3. **Alignment of Actions and Values:**
   - Authenticity demands consistency between your beliefs and behaviors. When actions contradict values, it creates inner conflict and dissatisfaction.

4. **Resilience in the Face of Pressure:**
   - Living authentically often means resisting external pressures to conform. Developing resilience and confidence in your worth helps you stay true to your values, even when faced with judgment or rejection.

Psychological Insights

- **Maslow's Self-Actualization:** Living authentically aligns with self-actualization, the highest tier in Maslow's hierarchy of needs.

It involves realizing your full potential and living in a way that reflects your deepest values.
- **Cognitive Dissonance:** When your actions conflict with your values, you experience discomfort known as cognitive dissonance. Resolving this by realigning your behavior with your beliefs fosters peace and authenticity.
- **Authenticity and Well-Being:** Studies reveal that authenticity enhances psychological well-being, self-esteem, and life satisfaction. Living authentically cultivates a sense of purpose and fulfillment.

Self-Actualization Excellence: Vince Lombardi

Vince Lombardi is an excellent example of someone who embodied the principles of **self-actualization** and authentic living in alignment with his deepest values. As one of the most celebrated football coaches in history, Lombardi not only achieved great success with his teams but also lived and led in a way that reflected his core beliefs about discipline, perseverance, and integrity.

Vince Lombardi's Alignment with Core Values

Lombardi's philosophy revolved around a relentless commitment to excellence. His famous quote, *"Perfection is not attainable, but if we chase perfection, we can catch excellence,"* encapsulates his drive to push both himself and his players toward their highest potential. This pursuit mirrors **Maslow's concept of self-actualization**, where individuals strive to realize their full capabilities. Lombardi believed that success wasn't just about winning games—it was about effort, character, and teamwork. His leadership demonstrated an authentic alignment between his values and his actions, as he consistently modeled and demanded the qualities he championed.

Living His Core Beliefs

Lombardi's authentic leadership style was evident in his emphasis on preparation and discipline. He believed in leaving no detail unchecked, and his meticulous approach to coaching reflected his dedication to the values of hard work and integrity. He famously stated, *"The quality of a person's life is in direct proportion to their commitment to excellence, regardless of their chosen field of endeavor."* For Lombardi, football was a platform for instilling life lessons about personal accountability, teamwork, and resilience.

A Self-Actualized Leader

Lombardi's ability to inspire others was rooted in his authenticity. He understood his purpose—not just as a coach but as a mentor and leader who helped others strive for greatness. His values-driven approach created a culture where players felt motivated to push beyond their limits, not just for the team but for their own growth. His ability to connect deeply with his players and align his strategies with his principles demonstrates how living authentically fosters both personal fulfillment and transformative impact on others.

Maslow's Self-Actualization in Lombardi's Legacy

Vince Lombardi's legacy exemplifies **Maslow's self-actualization** because he achieved mastery in his field while staying true to his beliefs. His life serves as a powerful reminder that living authentically—aligning one's actions with one's values—leads to enduring success and personal fulfillment. Lombardi's career wasn't just about football; it was about realizing potential, leading with integrity, and inspiring others to do the same. His story highlights how self-actualization can extend beyond individual achievement to leave a lasting impact on those around us.

Saintly Example: Mother Teresa

Mother Teresa's life epitomizes authentic living. She dedicated herself to serving the poorest and most vulnerable, embodying her values of compassion, humility, and love. Her commitment to living according to her faith and principles made her a global symbol of selflessness and kindness.

Mother Teresa's unwavering focus on her mission, even in the face of immense challenges, illustrates the power of authenticity. Her work was not about grand gestures but about living her values in everyday interactions, transforming lives through simple acts of kindness and unwavering commitment.

Mother Teresa, later canonized as Saint Teresa of Calcutta, stands as a saintly exemplar of aligning one's life with deeply held values. Her unwavering commitment to love, humility, and service defined not only her mission but also her essence as an individual. She believed that every human life, regardless of circumstance, deserved dignity and care, and she made it her life's work to embody that belief in every action she took.

In 1950, Mother Teresa founded the **Missionaries of Charity**, an organization devoted to serving "the poorest of the poor." Her values were not confined to words but were evident in her everyday actions—feeding the hungry, tending to the sick, and offering solace to the dying. She practiced what she preached, often working in the most destitute conditions alongside those she served. For her, authenticity meant not just recognizing suffering but actively alleviating it through small, meaningful acts of compassion. Her philosophy is encapsulated in her famous words: *"If you can't feed a hundred people, then feed just one."*

A deeply impactful story illustrates the saintly depth of her authenticity. When asked by a man how he could make a difference amid the overwhelming suffering in the world, she didn't suggest grand gestures but instead offered a simple, actionable step: *"Go out into the city early in the morning, find someone who is homeless and convince them they are loved. Give them hope."* For Mother Teresa, authentic living meant that love must be practical and immediate, capable of touching individual lives in ways that restore their sense of humanity. Her advice highlighted her belief in the ripple effect of small, sincere acts of kindness.

Despite her saintly reputation, Mother Teresa was candid about her personal struggles with doubt and spiritual darkness, as revealed in her private letters. Rather than diminishing her authenticity, these struggles showcased it. She did not shy away from acknowledging her vulnerabilities but embraced them as part of her human experience and journey of faith. By remaining steadfast in her mission, even amid internal challenges, she demonstrated that authenticity is about perseverance in living according to one's values, not about achieving perfection.

Mother Teresa's legacy is a testament to the power of living authentically with love as a guiding force. Her life continues to inspire people across the globe to align their actions with their values, showing that saintly greatness often begins with simple acts of compassion. By embracing her teachings and example, we are reminded that authenticity, paired with a selfless commitment to others, has the power to heal and transform the world.

Practical Steps to Live Authentically

1. **Clarify Your Values:**
   - Identify what is most important to you, such as compassion, integrity, or creativity. Let these values guide your decisions.

2. **Practice Vulnerability:**
   - Share your true thoughts and feelings with those you trust. Embrace openness as a way to build deeper connections.

3. **Set Boundaries:**
   - Protect your authenticity by saying no to situations or relationships that conflict with your values.

4. **Reflect and Realign:**
   - Regularly assess whether your actions align with your values. Make adjustments where needed to maintain integrity.

5. **Act with Purpose:**
   - ☼ Incorporate your values into daily life through intentional, meaningful actions. Even small steps can create a lasting impact.

Key Takeaways

- Living authentically bridges the gap between who you are and how you live, fostering fulfillment and inner peace.
- Self-awareness, vulnerability, and alignment are essential for authentic living.
- Resilience helps you overcome external pressures and remain true to your values.
- By living authentically, you inspire others to do the same, creating a ripple effect of kindness, purpose, and connection.

Mother Teresa's story reminds us that authenticity is not about perfection but about consistency and intention. Through her values-driven actions, she demonstrated that small, genuine gestures have the power to create profound change in the world. Living authentically invites us all to find our unique purpose and contribute meaningfully to the lives of others.

"The measure of who we are is what we do with what we have."
— *Vince Lombardi*

CHAPTER 11

Limitless Living: Becoming the Best Version of Yourself

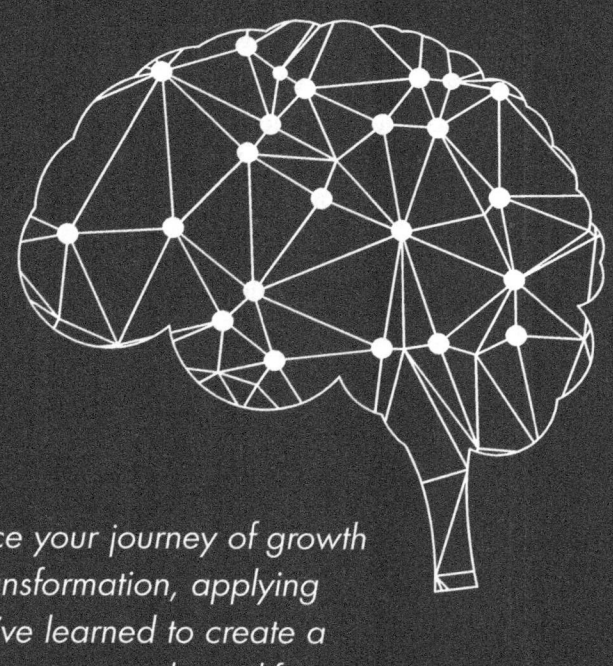

Embrace your journey of growth and transformation, applying all you've learned to create a fulfilling, purpose-driven life.

Limitless living is about transcending perceived barriers, embracing personal growth, and striving to become the best version of yourself. It involves adopting a growth mindset, aligning your actions with your values, and continuously learning from challenges and experiences. The journey to becoming your best self requires self-awareness, resilience, and the courage to push beyond comfort zones while remaining authentic to who you are. Limitless living doesn't mean perfection but rather ongoing progress and the pursuit of purpose, fulfillment, and meaningful impact.

A compelling example of limitless living is **Albert Einstein**, who is widely regarded as one of the greatest minds in history. As a child, Einstein struggled academically and was slow to speak, leading some teachers and peers to label him as "dull." This led to the misconception that he had a learning disability, though modern scholars suggest his challenges were more likely linked to differences in learning style or even traits of dyslexia or autism. Despite these early struggles, Einstein demonstrated an unparalleled ability to think abstractly and challenge conventional wisdom. His groundbreaking theory of relativity redefined the understanding of time, space, and energy, proving that limitations in one area do not preclude greatness in another.

Interestingly, Einstein's brilliance was paired with moments of absent-mindedness that made him relatable. Stories tell of him getting lost in his own neighborhood or misplacing household items because he was so immersed in his thoughts and ideas. This highlights an essential aspect of limitless living: embracing quirks and imperfections as part of the unique fabric of who you are. Einstein's ability to channel his focus into transformative discoveries rather than dwelling on his challenges serves as a reminder that extraordinary achievements are possible when you focus on your strengths and pursue your passions.

The key takeaway from Einstein's life is that limitless living begins with embracing your individuality and harnessing your unique gifts. Challenges and setbacks are part of the journey, but they can be reframed as stepping stones to innovation and success. By cultivating curiosity, resilience, and authenticity, anyone can unlock their potential and achieve extraordinary results, regardless of where they start.

Limitless Living: Embracing Infinite Potential

"Limitless living" represents a mindset and lifestyle rooted in the belief that your potential is boundless, and your possibilities are only limited by the constraints you impose on yourself. This concept involves actively pursuing personal growth, breaking through barriers, and embracing the courage to live authentically and purposefully. It's about choosing to see challenges as opportunities, stepping beyond comfort zones, and envisioning a life where continuous improvement and meaningful impact define your journey.

"If you always put limits on everything you do, physical or anything else, it will spread into your work and your life. There are no limits. There are only plateaus, and you must not stay there; you must go beyond them."
— *Bruce Lee*

Key Aspects of Limitless Living

1. Breaking Boundaries

Limitless living starts with rejecting self-imposed boundaries. It means challenging societal expectations, breaking free from limiting beliefs, and daring to think big. By reframing constraints as opportunities to innovate, individuals can transcend perceived limitations and explore paths they once thought unattainable. This mindset shifts the focus from "What if I fail?" to "What could I achieve if I try?"

2. Embracing a Growth Mindset

A growth mindset, as popularized by psychologist Carol Dweck, is essential to limitless living. It involves seeing every experience—success or failure—as an opportunity to learn and grow. Instead of fearing setbacks, those who embrace this mindset view challenges as tools for development, continuously improving their skills, knowledge, and resilience. This perspective empowers individuals to see their potential as ever-evolving rather than fixed.

3. Cultivating a Positive Attitude

Optimism is a cornerstone of limitless living. Maintaining a positive attitude, even in the face of adversity, fosters the belief that obstacles can be overcome. A positive outlook not only motivates you to persevere but also helps attract opportunities and connections that align with your goals. It enables you to approach life with curiosity and enthusiasm, qualities that are critical for navigating uncharted territory.

4. Living Intentionally

Intentional living requires aligning your actions with your values and long-term goals. By making deliberate choices about how you spend your time and energy, you ensure that your life reflects your true priorities. This focus minimizes distractions and allows you to channel your resources into pursuits that bring fulfillment and purpose. Intentional living is about being proactive rather than reactive, shaping your future instead of merely responding to circumstances.

5. Embracing Challenges

Limitless living thrives on the willingness to embrace challenges. Stepping outside your comfort zone is not only necessary for growth but also for discovering your true capabilities. Challenges are opportunities in disguise, pushing you to explore untapped potential and develop strengths you didn't know you had. Adopting this mindset transforms adversity into a stepping stone for progress and resilience.

Living Limitlessly in Action

Consider the story of **Helen Keller**, who, despite being blind and deaf, became a world-renowned author, activist, and speaker. Her ability to transcend immense physical and societal limitations exemplifies limitless living. Keller's life demonstrates how a growth mindset, intentional actions, and unwavering optimism can lead to extraordinary achievements. Her journey reminds us that barriers are often external manifestations of internal doubts, and overcoming them starts with changing our mindset.

Limitless living also applies to everyday moments. For example, someone choosing to learn a new skill in their 50s, stepping into a leadership role for the first time, or starting a business after a series of failures embodies this mindset. These actions require embracing uncertainty and believing that growth and success are possible at any stage of life.

The Essence of Limitless Living

Limitless living is not about perfection or never facing difficulties—it's about persisting with the belief that you can rise above any challenge. It's about striving to live a life where your actions align with your values, where learning and growth are continuous, and where you see every setback as a stepping stone to success. This mindset fuels the courage to dream big, take risks, and create a fulfilling life that reflects your highest aspirations. By living limitlessly, you not only transform your own life but inspire others to believe in their boundless potential

A **purpose-driven life** is a life lived with intentionality, focus, and a deep sense of meaning. It involves aligning your actions, decisions, and priorities with your core values, passions, and the unique contribution you wish to make in the world. Living a purpose-driven life fosters a sense of fulfillment and direction, motivating individuals to pursue goals that resonate deeply with their sense of identity and aspirations.

Key Characteristics of a Purpose-Driven Life

1. Clarity of Purpose

A purpose-driven life begins with understanding your "why." This involves identifying what gives your life meaning, such as serving others, creating something lasting, or advocating for a cause. Your purpose acts as a compass, guiding your choices and helping you stay focused on what truly matters.

2. Alignment with Values

Purpose-driven individuals live in harmony with their values. They ensure their actions, relationships, and pursuits reflect what they stand for, such as honesty, compassion, or creativity. This alignment fosters authenticity and strengthens their sense of integrity.

3. Contribution to Others

A key component of a purpose-driven life is contributing to the well-being of others. This might mean nurturing a family, building a business that empowers employees, volunteering, or pursuing work that benefits society. A sense of purpose often extends beyond oneself, creating a ripple effect of positivity and impact.

4. Resilience Through Challenges

Purpose provides a powerful source of motivation during difficult times. When challenges arise, a clear sense of purpose helps individuals persevere and maintain perspective, knowing their efforts contribute to something larger than themselves.

5. Continuous Growth and Learning

Living with purpose involves an ongoing commitment to self-improvement and learning. Purpose-driven individuals seek to grow their knowledge, skills, and emotional intelligence to better serve their goals and communities.

Benefits of a Purpose-Driven Life

1. Increased Well-Being

Studies have shown that individuals with a strong sense of purpose report higher levels of happiness, reduced stress, and better physical health.

Purpose gives life meaning, which contributes to overall well-being and satisfaction.

2. Enhanced Focus and Motivation

Knowing your purpose clarifies priorities, helping you focus on what truly matters and avoid distractions. This clarity fuels motivation and persistence, especially during setbacks.

3. Stronger Relationships

Purpose-driven people often form deeper connections with others who share similar values or goals. This creates supportive, meaningful relationships that enrich life.

4. Legacy and Fulfillment

A purpose-driven life leaves a lasting legacy. Whether through relationships, contributions, or achievements, living with purpose creates a sense of fulfillment and pride in the impact you've made.

Finding and Living Your Purpose

- **Reflect on Your Values:** Identify what matters most to you and let those values guide your decisions.
- **Pursue Your Passions:** Engage in activities or work that ignite your enthusiasm and creativity.
- **Serve Others:** Look for ways to make a positive impact in your community or the world.
- **Set Meaningful Goals:** Define clear, actionable steps that align with your purpose and bring you closer to your vision.
- **Stay Open to Growth:** Understand that purpose can evolve over time. Be willing to adapt and embrace new opportunities that resonate with your journey.

Conclusion:
Living Limitlessly with Purpose and Vision

Living limitlessly and with purpose requires a mindset that transcends self-imposed limitations, embraces personal growth, and prioritizes alignment with your values and aspirations. At its core, limitless living is about believing in the boundless opportunities life offers, even in the face of challenges. It's not about perfection or achieving every goal without setbacks, but about persistence, resilience, and the courage to evolve. Similarly, a purpose-driven life provides the focus and clarity to channel limitless energy toward meaningful goals that reflect your unique values.

Key Principles of Limitless Living

To live limitlessly is to view challenges as stepping stones, to consistently push beyond your comfort zones, and to maintain a growth mindset. By embracing new experiences, learning from failures, and staying optimistic, you unlock opportunities for innovation and success. Albert Einstein's journey, from struggling academically as a child to revolutionizing science, epitomizes this mindset. His life shows how embracing curiosity, channeling passions, and persisting through obstacles can lead to extraordinary achievements.

Purpose as a Guide:

Purpose-driven living enhances limitless potential by offering direction and meaning. Aligning your actions with your values ensures that your efforts resonate deeply and authentically, fueling motivation and resilience. Historical examples like Mother Teresa illustrate how purpose amplifies impact. Her commitment to serving the poorest of the poor, despite immense challenges, exemplifies how a clear purpose enables individuals to rise above adversity and create lasting change.

Practical Application for a Limitless and Purposeful Life:

- **Reflect on Your Values and Passions:** Regularly evaluate what matters most to you and align your decisions with those priorities.
- **Embrace Challenges:** View obstacles as opportunities for growth and resilience.
- **Take Incremental Steps:** Break big dreams into achievable goals, celebrating progress along the way.
- **Learn Continuously:** Commit to personal and professional growth through learning and self-reflection.
- **Serve Others:** Integrate contributions to others as part of your vision for a fulfilling life.

Final Thoughts: A Legacy of Limitless Living

Living limitlessly means choosing courage over complacency, progress over perfection, and authenticity over conformity. It means harnessing the lessons of the past, embracing the uncertainties of the future, and continually striving to become the best version of yourself. When combined with purpose, this mindset not only transforms your own life but also leaves a lasting impact on the world around you.

> *"The meaning of life is to find your gift. The purpose of life is to give it away."*
> — *Pablo Picasso*

CHAPTER 12

The Role of Emotional and Spiritual Intelligence – Navigating Relationships and Challenges

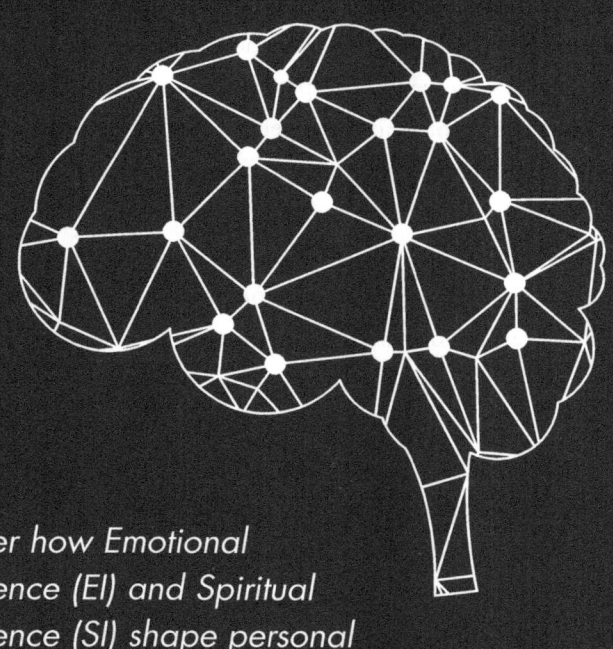

Discover how Emotional Intelligence (EI) and Spiritual Intelligence (SI) shape personal and professional growth, enhancing resilience, relationships, and the ability to overcome life's challenges with purpose and empathy.

EI or EQ stands for **Emotional Intelligence** or **Emotional Quotient**, referring to the ability to recognize, understand, and manage emotions effectively in oneself and others. Unlike IQ (Intelligence Quotient), which measures cognitive abilities, EQ focuses on emotional and social skills that play a critical role in interpersonal relationships, decision-making, and personal well-being.

The Role of Emotional Intelligence – Navigating Relationships and Challenges centers on the ability to recognize, understand, and manage emotions in oneself and others. Emotional Intelligence (EI or EQ) is a multifaceted skill that includes self-awareness, self-regulation, empathy, social skills, and motivation. This comprehensive understanding of emotions enhances the ability to navigate interpersonal relationships, adapt to change, and respond effectively to challenges. By mastering emotional intelligence, individuals can cultivate stronger connections, improve decision-making, and foster a sense of balance in both personal and professional spheres.

A cornerstone of emotional intelligence is **self-awareness**, the ability to recognize and understand your own emotions and their impact on your behavior. Self-awareness enables individuals to identify their emotional triggers and patterns, allowing them to respond to situations with clarity rather than reactivity. For example, someone with high self-awareness can recognize when stress is clouding their judgment and take proactive steps to regain focus. This self-insight not only improves personal decision-making but also lays the foundation for self-regulation, another critical aspect of EI. Self-regulation involves managing emotions constructively, staying calm under pressure, and navigating conflicts without escalation, which is essential for maintaining stability in challenging situations.

Empathy, the ability to understand and share the feelings of others, is another vital component of emotional intelligence. Empathy fosters deeper connections by allowing individuals to see the world through another person's perspective, creating trust and mutual respect. **Martin Luther King Jr.**, for example, exemplified empathy in his efforts to inspire social change. By addressing the pain, hopes, and dreams of a marginalized population, he connected with people on an emotional level, galvanizing them to work together toward justice and equality. His ability to tap into the emotions of others was a powerful tool for navigating relationships and inspiring collective action. This same principle applies to everyday interactions; when individuals approach conversations with empathy, they foster understanding and reduce conflict.

In professional settings, **emotional intelligence enhances leadership, teamwork, and adaptability**. Leaders with high EI can inspire and motivate their teams by recognizing individual strengths and addressing concerns with compassion and transparency. Teams that operate with emotional intelligence are better equipped to collaborate, resolve disputes, and maintain a positive work environment, even under pressure. Emotional intelligence also bolsters resilience by helping individuals view challenges as opportunities for growth rather than insurmountable obstacles. For instance, an emotionally intelligent leader faced with a failed project might focus on the lessons learned and encourage the team to approach future tasks with renewed determination. This mindset not only boosts morale but also drives continuous improvement, making emotional intelligence a cornerstone of long-term success.

In essence, emotional intelligence is a transformative skill that empowers individuals to navigate the complexities of relationships and challenges with grace and effectiveness. By developing self-awareness, empathy, and resilience, individuals can foster deeper connections, enhance personal and professional growth, and create environments where trust and collaboration thrive. Emotional intelligence is not a fixed trait but a dynamic capability that can be cultivated with practice, making it a powerful tool for anyone seeking to lead a more balanced, fulfilling life.

What is Emotional Intelligence?

Emotional Intelligence, a concept popularized by psychologist **Daniel Goleman**, involves five core components:

1. **Self-Awareness**: Recognizing and understanding your emotions and their impact on your behavior and decisions.

2. **Self-Regulation**: Managing your emotions constructively, avoiding impulsive reactions, and adapting to changing circumstances.
3. **Motivation**: Harnessing emotions to stay focused on goals, maintaining optimism, and persisting through challenges.
4. **Empathy**: Understanding and sharing the feelings of others, fostering connection and compassion.
5. **Social Skills**: Building and maintaining healthy relationships through effective communication, teamwork, and conflict resolution.

How Emotional Intelligence Navigates Relationships

1. **Strengthening Connections**: EI helps individuals relate to others on a deeper level by fostering empathy and understanding. For example, recognizing a friend's stress allows you to offer support in a meaningful way, strengthening the bond.
2. **Effective Communication**: Those with high EI express themselves clearly and listen actively, reducing misunderstandings and improving collaboration.
3. **Conflict Resolution**: Emotional intelligence enables individuals to navigate disagreements calmly, focusing on solutions rather than personal attacks, which preserves relationships and builds trust.

The Role of EI in Overcoming Challenges

1. **Stress Management**: High EI individuals are better equipped to handle stress, as they can identify their emotional triggers and use techniques like mindfulness or reframing to stay balanced.
2. **Resilience**: EI fosters the ability to recover from setbacks by encouraging a growth mindset and viewing failures as opportunities for learning.
3. **Adaptability**: Emotional intelligence enhances flexibility, helping individuals navigate change or uncertainty with composure.

A Great Example of Emotional Intelligence in Action

Abraham Lincoln stands as a profound example of emotional intelligence (EI) in leadership, showcasing his remarkable ability to remain calm under pressure and connect with people from diverse backgrounds. His presidency during one of America's most tumultuous periods, the Civil War, demanded exceptional emotional regulation, empathy, and interpersonal skills—all hallmarks of high EI.

Lincoln's Emotional Regulation

One of Lincoln's most defining traits was his ability to stay composed during crises. He often faced immense stress and opposition, yet he rarely allowed his emotions to dictate his actions or decisions. For example, during the Civil War, he navigated an often-fractious cabinet filled with individuals who had competing visions for the nation. Known as a "Team of Rivals," this group of advisors could have descended into dysfunction without Lincoln's steady and emotionally intelligent leadership. His capacity to listen patiently, defuse tension, and foster collaboration ensured that critical decisions were made with collective input rather than emotional discord.

Empathy as a Tool for Leadership

Lincoln's empathy was another critical aspect of his emotional intelligence. He was known for his deep compassion for others, which informed his leadership style and decisions. His famous Gettysburg Address, which honored fallen soldiers, reflected his ability to understand and articulate the grief and resolve of a nation at war. Beyond speeches, his personal interactions also demonstrated empathy. He often visited Union troops on the battlefield, listening to their stories and concerns, which not only boosted morale but also allowed him to stay connected to the realities of war. His empathetic approach helped bridge divides and foster unity in a nation torn apart by conflict.

Effective Communication and Influence

Lincoln's ability to communicate effectively was pivotal in his role as a leader. He possessed a unique talent for connecting with individuals from all walks of life, whether they were political adversaries, common citizens, or enslaved individuals seeking freedom. His speeches, letters, and personal interactions conveyed authenticity and humility, allowing him to build trust and influence even among those who initially opposed him. This ability to connect emotionally with others was key to his success in rallying the nation behind the abolition of slavery and the preservation of the Union.

Resilience in the Face of Adversity

Finally, Lincoln's resilience highlights his emotional intelligence. Throughout his life, he faced significant personal and professional setbacks, including the death of loved ones, electoral defeats, and a nation in turmoil. Despite these challenges, he maintained a forward-thinking mindset and remained focused on his vision of a united and free America. His ability to transform personal hardships into sources of strength and empathy made him a beacon of hope for others.

Abraham Lincoln's emotional intelligence was a cornerstone of his leadership, enabling him to navigate immense challenges, inspire a divided nation, and leave a legacy of unity and equality. His example serves as a powerful reminder of how emotional intelligence can transcend adversity and foster transformative change.

Developing Emotional Intelligence

Emotional intelligence is not fixed; it can be cultivated through deliberate practice. Here are steps to enhance your EI:

- **Practice Self-Reflection**: Regularly assess your emotions and their impact on your behavior.

- **Develop Empathy**: Make an effort to understand perspectives that differ from your own.
- **Improve Communication**: Use active listening, open body language, and clear expression of thoughts and feelings.
- **Learn Stress Management Techniques**: Engage in activities like meditation, deep breathing, or journaling to regulate emotions.
- **Seek Feedback**: Ask for constructive feedback from others to gain insights into how your emotions and behaviors affect them.

Why Emotional Intelligence Matters

Emotional Intelligence bridges the gap between intellectual ability and effective action. In a world where challenges and interpersonal dynamics are unavoidable, EI provides the tools to navigate these complexities with grace, resilience, and understanding. It empowers individuals to create meaningful relationships, lead with empathy, and adapt to life's ups and downs. Cultivating emotional intelligence is not just about personal success—it's about contributing positively to the world around you.

Examples of Emotional Intelligence in the Animal Kingdom

Emotional intelligence (EI) can be observed in the natural world, particularly in the social behaviors of animals. While animals may not possess the full spectrum of human emotional intelligence, many species exhibit traits that align with key aspects of EI, such as empathy, social awareness, emotional regulation, and the ability to manage relationships within their groups.

1. Empathy and Compassion

Elephants are renowned for their empathetic behaviors. They comfort distressed members of their herd by touching them with their trunks and even stand vigil over deceased companions, suggesting an awareness of the emotions of others. These behaviors demonstrate emotional attunement and a capacity to respond to the feelings of others, which are key components of empathy—a core aspect of emotional intelligence.

2. Social Awareness and Communication

Dolphins exhibit remarkable social intelligence. They form complex social bonds, cooperate with one another, and even display behaviors like assisting injured pod members. Dolphins also use intricate vocalizations to communicate and maintain relationships, showing an awareness of social dynamics within their pods.

3. Emotional Regulation

Primates such as chimpanzees and bonobos demonstrate the ability to regulate their emotions during social interactions. For example, they may reconcile after conflicts by grooming or embracing, showing an ability to manage their emotional responses to maintain harmony within their group. This behavior mirrors the human ability to repair relationships and manage social tension through emotional regulation.

4. Teamwork and Cooperation

Wolves exhibit emotional intelligence through their cooperative hunting strategies and structured social hierarchies. The pack works cohesively, with each member understanding their role and contributing to the group's success. Wolves also show loyalty and emotional bonds within their packs, ensuring group survival through collaboration and mutual support.

5. Parental Care and Nurturing

Birds such as penguins exhibit extraordinary dedication and nurturing behaviors, particularly in their roles as parents. Emperor penguins, for instance, endure extreme cold while taking turns keeping their eggs warm, a display of patience, cooperation, and devotion to their offspring. This nurturing behavior reflects a sense of responsibility and the emotional connection to their young.

Lessons from Nature for Human Emotional Intelligence

The natural world offers valuable lessons on emotional intelligence:

- **Empathy and Cooperation:** Animals demonstrate the power of working together for mutual benefit, reminding us that collaboration and understanding are essential for community success.
- **Conflict Resolution:** The ability of primates to reconcile after disputes highlights the importance of repairing relationships and fostering harmony.
- **Adaptability:** Many animals regulate their emotional responses to changing circumstances, showing resilience and resourcefulness—key elements of emotional intelligence in humans.

While animals may not have the same level of self-awareness or emotional complexity as humans, their behaviors reflect many of the fundamental principles of emotional intelligence. Observing these traits in nature can inspire us to deepen our understanding of emotions, enhance our relationships, and develop greater empathy and cooperation in our own lives. The natural world reminds us that emotional intelligence is not solely a human trait but a vital aspect of thriving within a community.

The story of the rhinoceros—its resilience through the epochs of time and its instinct to charge headfirst—offers a compelling metaphor for human behavior. While the **"Rhino Principle"** is often celebrated as a call to action, it also serves as an example of how unchecked emotional responses, a lack of reflection, or impulsivity can hinder emotional intelligence (EI). The rhino's boldness highlights both the potential benefits of proactive action and the pitfalls of acting without mindfulness or emotional regulation.

The Rhino Principle and Emotional Intelligence

The rhino's instinct to charge directly into obstacles mirrors how some people confront challenges: head-on, with single-minded determination. While this can be a strength in tackling procrastination or overcoming initial fear, it lacks the nuance of emotional intelligence. Emotional intelligence involves balancing decisiveness with self-awareness, empathy, and regulation. If a person acts like a rhino in every situation—charging ahead without assessing the emotional landscape—they risk alienating others, escalating conflicts, or making impulsive decisions that could lead to unintended consequences.

For instance, consider a workplace scenario where a team member encounters a disagreement. Adopting a "rhino" approach by addressing the conflict head-on without considering others' emotions or perspectives might resolve the issue quickly but leave lasting damage to relationships. Emotional intelligence would encourage a more measured approach: recognizing one's own emotions, understanding the perspectives of others involved, and using empathy to navigate the situation collaboratively.

Lessons from the Rhino: When Action Needs Mindfulness

The rhino's fearlessness reminds us of the importance of taking action, especially when fear or perfectionism paralyzes progress. For example, if you've been procrastinating on starting a new project, channeling the rhino's boldness can help overcome that inertia. However, emotional intelligence tempers this boldness with thoughtfulness. Before charging ahead, ask yourself:

- **What's the bigger picture?** Emotional intelligence involves assessing the long-term implications of your actions rather than acting impulsively.
- **How might others be affected?** Understanding the emotions and needs of those around you ensures your approach is constructive rather than destructive.

Without these considerations, the rhino's metaphor risks encouraging reactive, headstrong behavior that prioritizes immediate results over long-term harmony and growth.

A Balanced Approach: Combining Boldness with EI

The rhino's resilience and determination are admirable, but they are most effective when paired with emotional intelligence. Boldness becomes a strength when it is informed by:

- **Self-Awareness:** Recognizing when it's appropriate to charge forward and when to pause for reflection.
- **Empathy:** Considering how your actions might impact others and adapting accordingly.
- **Emotional Regulation:** Channeling the drive to act into purposeful, strategic efforts rather than impulsive reactions.

For example, if you've been procrastinating on having a difficult conversation with a friend or colleague, adopting the rhino's courage can help you take the first step. But instead of charging in, you might begin by understanding your own emotions, empathizing with the other person's perspective, and framing the discussion in a constructive, solution-oriented way. This balance ensures that boldness is guided by wisdom and care.

The Rhino Principle underscores the value of bold action but also serves as a cautionary tale about the dangers of acting without emotional intelligence. While fearlessness can help us tackle life's challenges, it must be tempered with self-awareness, empathy, and mindfulness to ensure that our actions lead to positive outcomes. By combining the rhino's strength with the insight of emotional intelligence, we can navigate relationships and challenges in a way that is both courageous and considerate, ensuring not only progress but also harmony and growth.

SQ vs. IQ and EQ: Spiritual Quotient (SQ), also referred to as Spiritual Intelligence

While **IQ** focuses on cognitive abilities and problem-solving, and **EQ** centers on understanding and managing emotions, **SQ** deals with deeper existential questions and values. It enables individuals to align their actions with their core beliefs and to act authentically in a complex, interconnected world.

Spiritual Quotient (SQ), also referred to as **Spiritual Intelligence**, is a concept that reflects an individual's ability to access deeper meanings, values, and purposes in life. SQ extends beyond cognitive intelligence (IQ) and emotional intelligence (EQ) to incorporate a sense of connection to something greater than oneself, whether that's a divine presence, nature, humanity, or universal truth.

Spiritual Quotient (SQ): Shaping Beliefs, Reality, and Achieving Limitless Expectations

Spiritual Quotient (SQ) represents a deeper dimension of intelligence that allows individuals to connect with their inner purpose, align their beliefs with their values, and cultivate resilience in the face of challenges. SQ empowers individuals to look beyond material goals, focusing on what brings fulfillment, meaning, and a sense of contribution. This intelligence is pivotal in shaping one's reality because it fosters a mindset rooted in purpose, gratitude, and interconnectedness. When individuals operate with a strong SQ, they can transcend limiting beliefs, embrace new perspectives, and navigate adversity with a profound sense of purpose. This transformation paves the way for achieving limitless expectations by empowering individuals to act authentically and courageously in pursuit of their goals.

SQ's ability to reshape beliefs and realities is evident in leaders who have overcome tremendous obstacles through their spiritual intelligence. Consider **Mahatma Gandhi**, who faced immense adversity while advocating for India's independence through nonviolence. Gandhi's deep sense of purpose and unwavering belief in truth and justice were the cornerstones of his SQ. Despite facing imprisonment and opposition, he remained steadfast, inspiring millions to align their actions with higher ideals. His spiritual intelligence not only enabled him to endure hardship but also unified diverse communities under a shared vision. Gandhi's example illustrates how SQ can transform daunting challenges into opportunities for societal change, demonstrating that when leaders connect with their higher purpose, they can achieve outcomes previously deemed impossible.

Another striking example is **Dr. Martin Luther King Jr.**, whose leadership during the Civil Rights Movement showcased extraordinary SQ. King's ability to see beyond the immediate struggles of racism and envision a future of equality and justice required profound spiritual insight. His speeches, such as "I Have a Dream," were imbued with a sense of hope, moral clarity, and a deep connection to universal values. These qualities not only motivated people to act courageously but also reshaped societal beliefs about justice and human dignity. King's SQ helped him navigate adversity, uniting communities in the pursuit of civil rights and equality. His life demonstrates that spiritual intelligence is a powerful tool for transforming both personal and collective realities, enabling individuals and leaders to achieve limitless expectations. By cultivating SQ, individuals can harness their inner strength, align their actions with their deepest values, and create a life of profound impact and fulfillment.

Key Aspects of SQ

1. **Self-Awareness**:
    - Recognizing your values, beliefs, and purpose in life.
    - Understanding how your spiritual or philosophical worldview shapes your decisions and actions.

2. **Transcendence**:
    - The ability to rise above immediate concerns to see a bigger picture.
    - Feeling connected to something larger, such as humanity, the universe, or a higher power.

3. **Inner Peace**:
    - Cultivating calmness and resilience, even in challenging situations.
    - Drawing strength from a sense of purpose or spiritual grounding.

4. **Compassion and Empathy**:
    - Demonstrating kindness and understanding toward others.
    - Seeing the interconnectedness of all life and acting with a sense of stewardship or service.

5. **Meaning-Making**:
    - Finding purpose and significance in experiences, including suffering and challenges.
    - Reflecting on life's questions such as "Why am I here?" or "What is my legacy?"

Measuring Spiritual Quotient

While SQ is less quantifiable than IQ or EQ, various tools and assessments attempt to gauge an individual's spiritual intelligence. These often involve self-reflection and exploration of values, ethics, and life purpose.

Why SQ Matters

- In a world of rapid change and uncertainty, SQ helps people maintain balance, make ethical decisions, and build meaningful connections.
- It bridges the gap between emotional well-being (EQ) and purpose-driven living, fostering holistic personal growth.

Enhancing your **Spiritual Quotient (SQ)** involves cultivating a deeper connection to yourself, others, and the larger purpose of your life. Here are practical ways to develop and strengthen your SQ:

1. Cultivate Self-Awareness

- **What to Do**: Reflect on your values, beliefs, and purpose in life. Journaling or meditation can help you uncover what truly matters to you.
- **Why It Matters**: Self-awareness is the foundation of spiritual intelligence. Understanding your inner motivations and convictions allows you to act authentically and with purpose.
- **Exercise**: Write a "Purpose Statement" that outlines your core values and the legacy you wish to leave behind.

2. Practice Mindfulness and Presence

- **What to Do**: Engage in activities that center your mind and bring awareness to the present moment, such as meditation, yoga, or mindful breathing.
- **Why It Matters**: Mindfulness enhances your ability to observe your thoughts and emotions without judgment, fostering inner peace and clarity.
- **Exercise**: Spend 5-10 minutes daily in silent reflection, focusing on your breath and letting go of distractions.

3. Engage in Meaningful Service

- **What to Do**: Contribute to your community or support causes aligned with your values. Volunteer, mentor, or help others in need.
- **Why It Matters**: Service shifts the focus from self to others, cultivating empathy and a sense of interconnectedness.
- **Exercise**: Choose a small act of kindness to perform daily, such as helping a colleague, donating to a cause, or simply listening deeply to someone.

4. Seek Connection with Nature

- **What to Do**: Spend time outdoors, appreciating the natural world. Activities like hiking, gardening, or simply observing a sunrise can help.
- **Why It Matters**: Nature fosters a sense of wonder and interconnectedness, reminding us of the larger systems that sustain life.
- **Exercise**: Spend at least 30 minutes a week in nature, reflecting on your relationship with the environment and the lessons it offers.

5. Pursue Lifelong Learning

- **What to Do**: Study spiritual, philosophical, or ethical teachings from diverse traditions. Explore books, podcasts, or courses that challenge your perspective.
- **Why It Matters**: Learning broadens your understanding of life's deeper questions and helps you develop a more inclusive and empathetic worldview.
- **Exercise**: Dedicate time each month to explore a new book, lecture, or documentary that expands your spiritual or philosophical horizons.

6. Foster Gratitude and Appreciation

- **What to Do**: Regularly reflect on the blessings in your life and express gratitude for them.
- **Why It Matters**: Gratitude shifts your focus from scarcity to abundance, enhancing emotional and spiritual well-being.
- **Exercise**: Keep a gratitude journal and list three things you are thankful for every day.

7. Develop a Regular Spiritual Practice

- **What to Do**: Establish routines that nurture your spiritual side, such as prayer, meditation, or contemplation.

- **Why It Matters**: Consistent practices strengthen your connection to your values, purpose, or higher power.
- **Exercise**: Dedicate a specific time each day to your practice, whether it's morning meditation, evening prayer, or quiet reflection.

8. Explore Your Inner Purpose

- **What to Do**: Engage in deep introspection to identify what gives your life meaning and aligns with your passions.
- **Why It Matters**: Understanding your purpose creates a guiding framework for your actions and decisions.
- **Exercise**: Reflect on questions like:
  - ☼ What brings me joy and fulfillment?
  - ☼ How can I use my strengths to serve others?
  - ☼ What legacy do I want to leave behind?

9. Embrace Forgiveness

- **What to Do**: Let go of grudges and practice forgiveness toward yourself and others.
- **Why It Matters**: Forgiveness fosters emotional freedom and strengthens your connection to others, clearing emotional blockages that hinder spiritual growth.
- **Exercise**: Write a letter (unsent) forgiving someone or yourself for past actions.

10. Meditate on Interconnectedness

- **What to Do**: Reflect on how your actions affect others and the world around you.
- **Why It Matters**: Recognizing interconnectedness deepens your empathy and sense of responsibility.

- **Exercise**: Spend time visualizing how small actions, like kindness or waste reduction, ripple outward to benefit others and the environment.

11. Stay Open to Growth

- **What to Do**: Accept that spiritual intelligence evolves and that challenges are opportunities for growth.
- **Why It Matters**: Openness helps you adapt, learn, and develop resilience in the face of life's complexities.
- **Exercise**: When faced with adversity, ask yourself:
  o What lesson can I learn from this?
  o How can this experience help me grow?

By incorporating these practices into your daily life, you can enhance your **Spiritual Quotient** and cultivate a deeper, more meaningful connection with yourself, others, and the world

Connecting Within and Beyond: Harnessing Spiritual Quotient for Meaning, Peace, and Purpose

Spiritual Quotient (SQ) offers individuals a profound pathway to cultivate a deeper connection with themselves, others, and the world around them. By nurturing one's SQ, a person develops the ability to explore questions of meaning, purpose, and interconnectedness. This deeper awareness allows them to approach life's challenges with clarity and inner strength, fostering empathy and a sense of unity with others. Through practices like prayer, meditation, and reflection, SQ enables individuals to transcend their personal limitations and tap into a broader sense of the divine or universal wisdom, grounding their actions in love, compassion, and faith.

Many of life's challenges cannot be resolved through logical reasoning or external solutions alone. In such moments, turning to a higher power can provide emotional resolution and peace. A simple prayer, such as "God, please put your hand on my shoulder and give me peace," reflects an act of surrender, an acknowledgment that some burdens are too heavy to bear alone. The Bible provides powerful examples of this divine intervention. Jesus calming the storm on the Sea of Galilee illustrates how faith can bring peace to turbulent circumstances. Similarly, the story of the silver coin found in the fish's mouth teaches us to trust in divine providence when faced with seemingly impossible situations. These moments emphasize the importance of relying on a spiritual solution when no other resolution is within reach, highlighting the power of faith and trust in a higher authority.

Leaders throughout history have demonstrated the power of SQ in overcoming adversity and fostering meaningful connections. Mother Teresa, for example, relied on her deep faith and unwavering spiritual commitment to serve the poorest of the poor, inspiring countless individuals to see the value of compassion and selfless service. Similarly, Archbishop Desmond Tutu drew strength from his spirituality to lead efforts against apartheid in South Africa, preaching forgiveness, reconciliation, and unity even in the face of profound division and injustice. Both leaders exemplify how SQ fosters resilience, empathy, and the ability to inspire transformative change. By cultivating SQ, individuals can anchor themselves in a sense of purpose and divine guidance, finding the strength to navigate life's storms and the wisdom to see challenges as opportunities for spiritual growth and connection.

A Conclusion on the Power of Spiritual Quotient (SQ) and Emotional Intelligence (EQ): Cultivating Meaning, Peace, and Limitless Potential

Spiritual Quotient (SQ) and Emotional Intelligence (EQ) offer complementary pathways to personal growth, meaningful connections, and profound transformation. Together, they enable individuals to align their actions with their core values while fostering empathy, resilience, and a deep sense of purpose. SQ provides the framework for exploring questions of meaning and interconnectedness, while EQ equips us to navigate emotions, relationships, and challenges with grace and understanding. This harmonious integration of spiritual insight and emotional awareness forms a powerful foundation for living authentically and effectively.

Both SQ and EQ play vital roles in guiding us through life's most challenging moments. When logical solutions fall short, and emotions feel overwhelming, SQ encourages us to turn inward and seek support from a higher power. A simple prayer, such as "God, please put your hand on my shoulder and give me peace," reflects an act of surrender, acknowledging that some burdens are too heavy to bear alone. Similarly, EQ empowers us to identify and regulate emotions, transforming fear or frustration into clarity and action. Biblical examples, like Jesus calming the storm or finding the coin in the fish's mouth, show how faith and emotional composure together can provide solutions and peace in turbulent circumstances. These principles remind us that inner balance and trust in something greater can transform adversity into growth.

History abounds with examples of leaders who exemplified the power of SQ and EQ in overcoming obstacles and inspiring change. Dr. Martin Luther King Jr., for instance, drew upon his faith and emotional insight to connect with diverse audiences, articulate a vision of justice, and inspire peaceful resistance. His SQ provided him with a sense of divine purpose, while his EQ enabled him to navigate the complex emotions of a nation in turmoil, fostering unity and hope. Similarly, Mahatma Gandhi combined spiritual conviction with emotional awareness to lead a nonviolent movement that reshaped the course of history. These leaders demonstrate how SQ and EQ together create the capacity to navigate personal and societal challenges with wisdom and compassion.

By cultivating both SQ and EQ, individuals unlock their potential for limitless growth and fulfillment. SQ deepens our connection to meaning and purpose, while EQ enhances our ability to understand and manage emotions, fostering deeper relationships and resilience. Together, they create a balanced, dynamic approach to navigating life's complexities, enabling us to thrive in our personal lives and contribute positively to the world. With spiritual intelligence as our compass and emotional intelligence as our toolkit, we are empowered to embrace challenges, nurture connections, and transform both ourselves and the world around us.

The world is yearning for a collective embrace of empathy, understanding, and purposeful action. A greater good begins with each of us, in small daily choices to uplift others, challenge injustice, and foster connection.

When individuals tap into their Emotional Intelligence (EQ) to navigate relationships with care, and their Spiritual Quotient (SQ) to align actions with deeper purpose, they contribute to a more harmonious and compassionate world. These ripple effects of kindness and conscious living can transform communities and inspire global change.

The journey toward the greater good is not reserved for leaders or visionaries—it's in every smile shared, every bridge built, and every act of love extended. Together, through unity and purpose, we can illuminate a path where humanity thrives, not just survives.

"True wisdom lies in the harmony between our inner essence and the vast universe around us—where seeking meaning within illuminates the path to peace, purpose, and profound connection with all that exists."

CHAPTER 13

The Energy of Gratitude: Transforming Your Outlook Through Appreciation

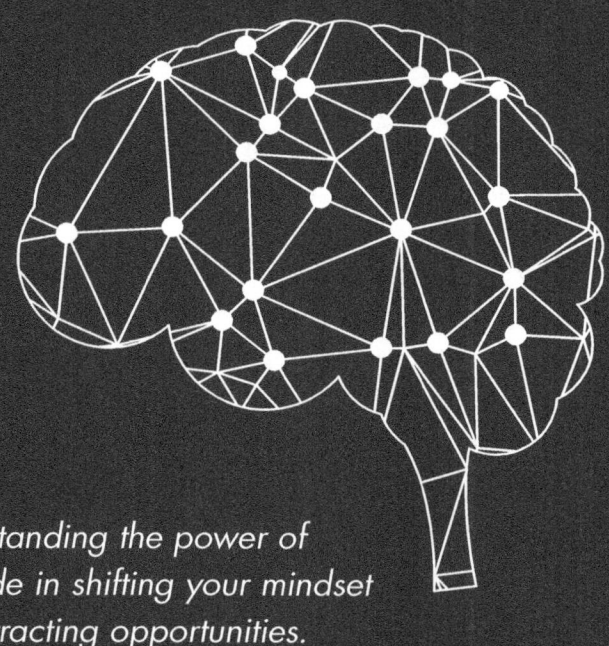

Understanding the power of gratitude in shifting your mindset and attracting opportunities.

The Energy of Gratitude: Transforming Your Outlook Through Appreciation

Gratitude is a powerful emotional and psychological practice that shifts focus from what we lack to what we have, fostering a sense of abundance and contentment. It involves actively recognizing and appreciating the positive aspects of life, no matter how small, and expressing thanks for them. The "energy of gratitude" refers to the transformative effect this practice can have on an individual's mindset, relationships, and overall well-being.

The practice of gratitude goes beyond mere acknowledgment; it involves a shift in perspective that can alter how we experience the world. When we consciously focus on what we are grateful for, our brains are primed to notice more positive occurrences, reinforcing a cycle of appreciation and joy. Neuroscience has shown that practicing gratitude increases activity in the brain's reward system, releasing feel-good neurotransmitters like dopamine and serotonin. This not only enhances mood but also builds resilience, helping individuals navigate life's challenges with greater optimism and strength.

Gratitude also serves as a powerful social connector. Expressing appreciation to others strengthens bonds and fosters mutual respect and understanding. Relationships thrive when people feel valued and acknowledged. For example, simply thanking a friend for their support can deepen trust and create a stronger emotional connection. Gratitude's ripple effects extend beyond individual relationships, influencing entire communities by promoting kindness and empathy.

Additionally, gratitude has profound effects on physical health. Studies suggest that individuals who regularly practice gratitude experience better sleep, lower stress levels, and improved immune function. Gratitude encourages a holistic sense of well-being, where emotional, mental, and physical health are interconnected and mutually reinforced. By cultivating gratitude, we create a foundation for a more balanced and fulfilling life, where even the smallest joys are celebrated as integral parts of our journey.

Key Psychological Concepts of Gratitude

1. Positive Psychology:

Gratitude is a cornerstone of positive psychology, a field that studies what contributes to human happiness and flourishing. Researchers like Dr. Robert Emmons have found that practicing gratitude can increase happiness, reduce depression, and improve resilience.

2. Cognitive Reframing:

Gratitude helps reframe situations, allowing individuals to see opportunities rather than obstacles. By focusing on what is going well, people can shift their perspective from scarcity to abundance, cultivating optimism and hope.

3. Neuroplasticity:

Regularly practicing gratitude rewires the brain. Gratitude activates the brain's reward system, releasing neurotransmitters like dopamine and serotonin, which contribute to feelings of happiness and well-being.

4. Emotional Regulation:

Gratitude encourages emotional balance, helping individuals manage stress and negativity. When gratitude becomes a habit, it promotes calmness and reduces the impact of daily challenges.

The Transformative Power of Gratitude

1. Shifts Focus:

Gratitude shifts the focus from what's missing to what's present, reducing envy, anxiety, and dissatisfaction. This redirection of energy promotes a sense of sufficiency and peace.

2. Improves Relationships:

Expressing gratitude strengthens relationships by fostering mutual respect and connection. A simple "thank you" can create a ripple effect of positivity, deepening bonds with friends, family, and colleagues.

3. Enhances Resilience:

Grateful individuals tend to cope better with adversity. By appreciating small wins and positive aspects, even during tough times, they maintain a solution-oriented outlook.

4. Boosts Physical Health:

Studies suggest that gratitude is linked to better sleep, lower blood pressure, and improved immune function. Feeling appreciative can reduce the physical toll of stress on the body.

Practicing Gratitude: Practical Strategies

1. Gratitude Journaling:

Write down three things you're grateful for each day. Over time, this practice trains your brain to focus on positives and enhances emotional well-being.

2. Express Appreciation:

Take time to thank someone sincerely, whether through a letter, a call, or in person. Expressing gratitude strengthens your connection to others and fosters positivity in your relationships.

3. Gratitude Meditation:

Spend a few moments reflecting on the things you appreciate. Visualization and mindfulness can deepen feelings of gratitude and calm.

4. Shift Language:

Incorporate gratitude into your daily speech. For example, instead of saying, "I have to," say, "I get to." This simple reframe turns obligations into opportunities.

Historical Example: Cicero's Enduring Wisdom

The **Roman philosopher Cicero** once remarked, *"Gratitude is not only the greatest of virtues but the parent of all others."* Cicero understood the profound role gratitude plays in shaping character and fostering harmony in society. In his writings, he emphasized that gratitude cultivates humility, strengthens relationships, and inspires acts of generosity.

Cicero's belief in gratitude as a foundational virtue remains relevant today. His reflections remind us that gratitude is not just a personal practice but a societal force. It builds bridges between people, fostering trust and mutual respect, and creates a ripple effect of positivity and connection that uplifts communities.

The Ripple Effect of Gratitude

Gratitude doesn't just benefit the individual—it creates a ripple effect. When you express appreciation, you inspire others to adopt a grateful mindset, fostering a culture of positivity and mutual support. This collective energy can transform relationships, workplaces, and communities.

Gratitude for Nature's Symbiotic Relationships: A Reflection on Interdependence

Human existence is intricately tied to the natural world in ways that often go unnoticed, yet these connections are vital for our survival and well-being. Expressing gratitude for these symbiotic relationships not only deepens our appreciation for nature but also fosters a sense of stewardship and responsibility. The natural world operates as a harmonious system, where each component plays a role in maintaining balance, often offering benefits to humanity without expectation. Recognizing these gifts encourages us to live in alignment with nature, respecting the delicate equilibrium that sustains us all.

Analogies of Nature's Gifts and Symbiosis

1. The Spiders and Insects

Without spiders, the world would face an overwhelming population of insects, including those that spread disease or destroy crops. Spiders, often misunderstood and even feared, are silent guardians of balance, acting as nature's pest control. Like an unseen workforce, they tirelessly maintain an equilibrium that benefits humanity. This relationship reminds us to appreciate even the smallest and least glamorous contributors to the natural world.

2. The Sun and the Sky

The sun and the sky exemplify generosity in their purest form. The sun provides warmth and light, enabling photosynthesis, which fuels the entire food chain. Without its energy, plants could not grow, oxygen would not be produced, and life would cease to exist. The sky complements the sun's work by delivering rain, nourishing crops, and replenishing water sources. Together, these elements of nature create a cycle of sustenance that underpins human existence—a partnership that silently ensures our survival.

3. The Bees and Pollination

Bees are tiny yet essential players in the web of life. Their role in pollination is crucial for the growth of fruits, vegetables, and flowers. Without bees, food production would drastically decline, leading to widespread famine. Their diligent work serves as a reminder of the interconnectedness of life and the importance of preserving biodiversity. Bees are nature's messengers of abundance, teaching us to value even the smallest contributors to the ecosystem.

4. The Forest and the Air

Forests, often called the "lungs of the Earth," absorb carbon dioxide and release oxygen, ensuring breathable air for all living creatures. Trees provide shade, regulate temperatures, and protect against soil erosion. In return, humans and animals contribute to forests by dispersing seeds and maintaining their growth. This mutual relationship exemplifies a symbiosis where giving and receiving occur in seamless harmony.

5. The Oceans and Weather Systems

The vast oceans regulate climate, absorb carbon dioxide, and provide food for billions of people. Their currents influence weather patterns, creating rain systems that nourish land ecosystems. Like a pulse that connects the planet, the oceans remind us of the interconnectedness of all life forms and the gratitude we owe to these unseen systems that shape our existence.

Lessons from Nature's Generosity

Nature's symbiotic relationships demonstrate a profound lesson in interdependence. Every element of the natural world, no matter how small or seemingly insignificant, plays a role in the greater balance of life. Humans, too, are part of this intricate web and benefit immensely from these connections. Expressing gratitude for these relationships is not only an acknowledgment of our reliance on nature but also a call to action to protect and nurture it in return.

For example:

- The selfless work of earthworms, which aerate soil and enhance fertility, enables crops to grow and sustain life.

- The fungi that form symbiotic relationships with tree roots facilitate nutrient absorption, ensuring forest health and resilience.
- Even the microorganisms in the soil and our own digestive systems highlight how unseen allies contribute to life and health.

Conclusion: A Mindset of Gratitude and Responsibility

Gratitude for nature's gifts encourages a mindset of reverence and responsibility. When we pause to recognize the silent, selfless work of the natural world, we not only deepen our appreciation but also foster a sense of duty to preserve and protect it. By drawing inspiration from the symbiotic relationships in nature, humans can learn to live harmoniously with the environment, ensuring that the cycles of giving and receiving continue for generations to come. Let us honor the natural world by cultivating gratitude, practicing sustainability, and acting as stewards of the incredible system that sustains us all.

What Does Gratitude Feel Like?

Gratitude is a deeply emotional state that resonates across multiple dimensions of our lives. It can evoke feelings of thankfulness, humility, and connection, reminding us of the positive aspects of our experiences. When you feel grateful, it's often accompanied by:

1. **Thankfulness and Humility**: A sense of appreciation for the efforts, circumstances, or people that have contributed to your well-being.
2. **Positivity and Peace**: A lighter emotional state, reducing stress and fostering a sense of calm or joy.
3. **Connectedness**: Gratitude often creates a sense of unity and understanding with others, enhancing your bond with those who have enriched your life.

For example, someone reflecting on a kind gesture from a friend may feel humbled and blessed, recognizing the value of the connection they share. Gratitude is not just an abstract concept; it's a tangible emotion that encourages us to dwell on life's gifts, large or small.

The Benefits of Gratitude

Gratitude has far-reaching effects, influencing both emotional well-being and physical health. It's not merely a fleeting feeling but a practice with measurable outcomes that improve the quality of life:

1. Improved Mood

Gratitude has been linked to increased levels of happiness and optimism. By focusing on what's good in life, gratitude shifts attention away from negative thoughts, fostering a positive outlook.

2. Enhanced Relationships

Expressing gratitude strengthens bonds, whether with friends, family, or romantic partners. It shows appreciation and reinforces trust and commitment, deepening the connection between individuals.

3. Increased Resilience

Gratitude can act as a buffer against stress, helping people recover more effectively from challenging or traumatic experiences. It encourages a focus on growth and positive outcomes, even in adversity.

4. Better Sleep

Reflecting on the day's blessings before bed can promote relaxation, helping you fall asleep faster and stay asleep longer.

5. More Kindness

Feeling grateful often inspires people to pay it forward, increasing acts of kindness and helpfulness. Gratitude fosters empathy, encouraging individuals to support and uplift others.

How Can You Practice Gratitude?

Gratitude is a skill that grows with practice. By cultivating a habit of appreciation, you can train your mind to focus on the positive aspects of life. Here are some ways to integrate gratitude into your daily routine:

1. Daily Reflection

Take a moment each day to reflect on what you're grateful for. This could include big accomplishments, small pleasures, or the simple fact of being alive.

2. Notice Small Blessings

Gratitude doesn't have to stem from monumental events. Appreciate the warmth of the sun, the laughter of a child, or the aroma of your morning coffee.

3. Express Gratitude

Tell people you appreciate them. Write a thank-you note, send a thoughtful text, or verbally acknowledge someone's impact on your life.

4. Keep a Gratitude Journal

Regularly jotting down things you're thankful for helps solidify the habit. Aim to write about three positive experiences each day.

5. Mindful Moments

Practice mindfulness to stay present and fully appreciate the moment you're in. Gratitude can flourish when you're attuned to your surroundings.

Cultivating Gratitude: A Life-Changing Perspective

Gratitude transforms how we view the world and interact with it. It acts as a bridge, connecting us to the good in our lives and encouraging us to share that positivity with others. As Roman philosopher Cicero once said, *"Gratitude is not only the greatest of virtues but the parent of all others."* By practicing gratitude, we unlock the potential for greater joy, stronger relationships, and a life imbued with meaning and purpose. Whether through daily reflections, acts of kindness, or appreciating the beauty of the world around us, gratitude offers a pathway to a more fulfilling and harmonious existence.

Conclusion: The Energy of Gratitude – A Transformative Practice

Gratitude is a profound force that has the power to reshape how we perceive and experience life. It allows us to shift our focus from what is lacking to what is abundant, fostering a mindset of appreciation, resilience, and connection. Gratitude not only enhances emotional and physical well-being but also deepens our relationships, strengthens communities, and inspires us to give back. It transforms ordinary moments into extraordinary blessings and infuses our lives with a sense of purpose and joy.

When we cultivate gratitude, we embrace a life enriched by perspective and balance. The natural world offers countless analogies to remind us of the interdependence that sustains life—spiders keeping insect populations in check, the sun warming the earth, and bees pollinating crops that nourish us. These gifts from nature, freely given, teach us that gratitude is not just an emotional response but a responsibility to cherish and protect what sustains us. In recognizing these symbiotic relationships, we learn to live in harmony with the world around us, fostering a sense of stewardship and interconnectedness.

Gratitude also compels us to action, encouraging us to express appreciation and acknowledge the contributions of others. From the simple act of thanking a friend to the deeper commitment of serving a community, gratitude builds bridges that enhance trust and compassion. It creates a ripple effect, spreading positivity far beyond the individual, touching the lives of those around us and fostering a culture of kindness and mutual respect.

As Cicero wisely stated, "Gratitude is not only the greatest of virtues but the parent of all others." This timeless truth reminds us that gratitude is not just a fleeting emotion but a way of living—a cornerstone of a fulfilling life. By practicing gratitude daily, we open ourselves to the beauty of the present moment, strengthen our resilience against adversity, and cultivate a perspective that sees challenges as opportunities for growth. Let us all make gratitude a guiding principle, allowing it to illuminate our paths and transform our outlook as we journey through life.

"Gratitude turns what we have into enough and more. It turns denial into acceptance, chaos into order, confusion into clarity. It makes sense of our past, brings peace for today, and creates a vision for tomorrow."
— Melody Beattie

CHAPTER 14

Limitless Horizons — Expanding Your Vision Beyond the Impossible

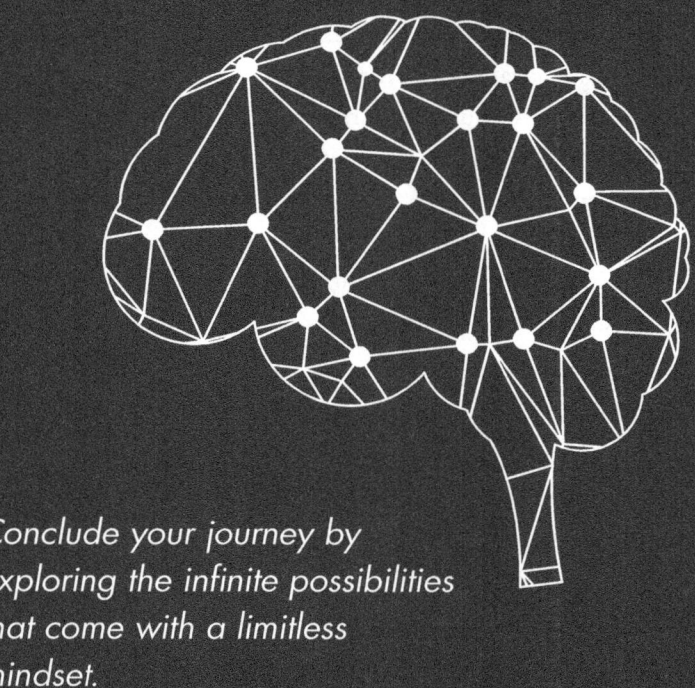

Conclude your journey by exploring the infinite possibilities that come with a limitless mindset.

Limitless Horizons – Expanding Your Vision Beyond the Impossible delves into the profound idea of transcending self-imposed and societal limitations to reach heights once thought unattainable. This philosophy invites individuals to reimagine their potential, breaking free from the constraints of conventional thinking and daring to explore new paths. By fostering a mindset that embraces boldness, innovation, and resilience, Limitless Horizons challenges us to envision a future where possibilities are as vast as our imagination.

At the core of this concept lies the principle of visionary thinking—an ability to see opportunities where others see obstacles. This requires cultivating a mindset that is not only growth-oriented but also unafraid to confront uncertainty. Visionaries such as the Wright brothers or contemporary pioneers like Elon Musk exemplify this philosophy. These individuals did not merely aim to solve existing problems but sought to redefine what was achievable, proving that breakthroughs often come from challenging the status quo and daring to ask, "What if?" Their stories remind us that expanding horizons begins with the courage to dream beyond the ordinary.

The journey toward Limitless Horizons is also rooted in action. Vision without execution remains a mere fantasy. To achieve what seems impossible, one must combine imagination with purposeful effort. Bold action requires calculated risk-taking, resilience in the face of setbacks, and an unwavering commitment to growth. For example, **SpaceX's** early failures in rocket launches did not deter its mission; instead, they served as learning opportunities that paved the way for its historic success. This underscores the idea that each step forward, even when fraught with challenges, contributes to an expanded vision of what is possible.

Moreover, Limitless Horizons emphasize the importance of collaboration and inspiration. Surrounding oneself with individuals who challenge conventional thinking and support audacious goals fosters an environment ripe for innovation. Communities that share a collective vision of boundless opportunity amplify individual efforts, creating momentum that transcends personal limitations. Whether through mentorship, partnerships, or shared experiences, these connections underscore the interdependence of human potential and highlight how expansive visions often thrive in collective environments.

By embracing the philosophy of Limitless Horizons, individuals open the door to extraordinary transformation—both for themselves and for the world around them. This concept calls for a shift in mindset, where constraints are seen not as barriers but as opportunities to innovate and grow. It is a reminder that when we dare to push beyond perceived boundaries, we unlock the potential for remarkable achievements that redefine what is possible.

Limitless Horizons – Expanding Your Vision Beyond the Impossible explores the transformative concept of pushing beyond perceived boundaries to imagine, achieve, and create futures that once seemed unattainable. This philosophy challenges individuals to break free from conventional constraints, cultivate visionary thinking, and embrace bold action to redefine what is possible.

The Core of Limitless Horizons

At its heart, the idea of Limitless Horizons is about expanding the scope of what you believe you can accomplish. It invites individuals to shift their perspective from what is realistic to what is possible, grounded in the belief that imagination, determination, and effort can overcome even the greatest obstacles. By embracing this mindset, you can transcend self-imposed limitations and tap into untapped potential, achieving outcomes that others may deem impossible.

Aligning with a Growth Mindset

The foundation of Limitless Horizons is closely tied to the concept of a growth mindset, as introduced by psychologist **Carol Dweck**. A growth mindset emphasizes that abilities and intelligence can be developed through dedication and hard work. This perspective encourages individuals to view challenges as opportunities to expand their skillset and redefine their limits.

Limitless Horizons takes this further by applying visionary thinking—not only striving for improvement but also imagining entirely new possibilities that transcend current capabilities or circumstances.

Historical and Modern Examples of Expanding Horizons

The **Wright brothers**, for instance, defied the long-held belief that humans were forever earthbound by designing and flying the first powered airplane. Remarkably, they accomplished this groundbreaking feat despite having no formal background in aviation or engineering. As bicycle makers from Dayton, Ohio, they were dismissed by academia and experts of their time, who believed that significant breakthroughs in aviation required extensive scientific credentials and institutional support. Undeterred, the Wright brothers leveraged their mechanical skills, creativity, and relentless determination to solve the problems of controlled flight.

Their audacious vision not only revolutionized transportation but also expanded humanity's ability to connect across great distances. By drawing from their experiences with bicycles—understanding balance, wind resistance, and mechanical efficiency—they approached aviation with a fresh perspective, unencumbered by conventional thinking. Their success at Kitty Hawk in 1903 proved that what once seemed impossible could become reality through perseverance, ingenuity, and the willingness to challenge the status quo.

Ironically, the very resistance the Wright brothers had to overcome in their pursuit of flight mirrors the principle that enables an airplane to achieve lift and soar through the skies. Just as an aircraft must face the wind to generate the lift necessary for flight, life often requires us to confront challenges and use them as a force to propel us forward. Like an airplane heading into the wind, embracing resistance and adversity can provide the momentum needed to rise above obstacles and reach new heights.

The Wright brothers' story is a testament to the power of pursuing bold ideas, even when the odds and societal expectations are stacked against you. Their journey reminds us that greatness often comes from outside traditional pathways and that innovation requires not only skill but also the courage to dream beyond the limits imposed by others. Their legacy continues to inspire generations to redefine what is possible, turning skepticism into awe and innovation into reality. In modern times, figures like **Dr. Mae Jemison**, the first African-American woman in space, exemplify Limitless Horizons through her groundbreaking work in science and exploration. Beyond her historic achievements with NASA, Dr. Jemison has consistently championed the integration of science, technology, and the arts, emphasizing that innovation comes from broad perspectives and bold ideas. Her vision of creating a more inclusive and multidisciplinary approach to solving global challenges demonstrates how expanding horizons requires not only technical skill but also the courage to imagine a better future for all.

Visionaries like **Nikola Tesla** also epitomize the spirit of limitless possibilities. Tesla's pioneering work in electricity and wireless communication laid the foundation for many modern technologies, including the alternating current (AC) system that powers much of our world today. Despite facing skepticism and financial difficulties, Tesla's relentless pursuit of his ideas and his ability to think beyond conventional limits showcase the transformative power of visionary thinking. His story reminds us that pushing beyond perceived boundaries often requires resilience, creativity, and an unwavering belief in the potential of one's ideas.

These examples underscore a universal truth: Limitless Horizons begin with the willingness to reimagine what is possible and the determination to act on those visions. Whether through aviation, space exploration, or groundbreaking scientific discoveries, history proves that humanity's greatest achievements arise when individuals dare to challenge the status quo and expand the scope of human potential. By adopting this mindset, we can continue to redefine the impossible and inspire future generations to pursue their own extraordinary horizons.

The Role of Imagination and Bold Action

Limitless Horizons also emphasizes the synergy between imagination and bold action. Visionary achievements require not only the ability to dream but also the courage to take the first step, even in the face of uncertainty. Expanding your horizons involves calculated risk-taking, resilience in the face of setbacks, and the relentless pursuit of your goals. It's about refusing to settle for mediocrity and daring to explore uncharted territories.

How to Expand Your Horizons

1. **Challenge Assumptions**: Identify and question limiting beliefs about what you can achieve. Reframe obstacles as opportunities for innovation.
2. **Visualize Big Goals**: Use visualization to imagine success beyond your current reality. Create a vivid mental image of the life or achievement you aspire to.
3. **Surround Yourself with Visionaries**: Engage with individuals and communities that challenge you to think bigger and inspire you with their own limitless visions.
4. **Take Incremental Steps**: While the vision may be vast, progress begins with small, actionable steps that build momentum.
5. **Embrace Failure as a Teacher**: Understand that failure is not an endpoint but a valuable part of growth. Use it as feedback to refine your approach.

The Legacy of Limitless Horizons

Embracing Limitless Horizons not only transforms individual lives but also contributes to societal progress. By daring to think beyond the impossible, we drive innovation, create new possibilities, and inspire others to reimagine their own potential. This concept is a call to courage, creativity, and the unyielding pursuit of a brighter future—one where the horizon is not a limit but a starting point. By embracing the philosophy of Limitless Horizons, individuals open the door to extraordinary transformation—both for themselves and for the world around them. This concept calls for a shift in mindset, where constraints are seen not as barriers but as opportunities to innovate and grow. It is a reminder that when we dare to push beyond perceived boundaries, we unlock the potential for remarkable achievements that redefine what is possible.

Conclusion: Limitless Horizons – Expanding Your Vision Beyond the Impossible

Limitless Horizons inspire us to reimagine what is possible, encouraging us to transcend perceived barriers and unlock our full potential. By challenging conventional thinking and daring to dream big, this philosophy pushes us to expand the scope of our ambitions and redefine what success means. Whether through groundbreaking innovation, personal transformation, or societal progress, Limitless Horizons serve as a powerful reminder that the only true limits are those we impose on ourselves.

At its core, this concept teaches us that imagination and bold action are inseparable forces. Vision alone is not enough; it must be paired with courage, resilience, and an unwavering commitment to progress. As history has shown, from the Wright brothers' first flight to Dr. Mae Jemison's pioneering work in space exploration, greatness arises when individuals refuse to be confined by what others deem impossible. Their stories serve as enduring examples of how limitless thinking leads to breakthroughs that shape the world.

To embrace Limitless Horizons in your own life, begin by challenging your assumptions about what you can achieve. Visualize a future where your goals are no longer restricted by fear or doubt, and take intentional steps toward that vision. Surround yourself with people and ideas that inspire growth, and remember that setbacks are not failures—they are lessons that refine your path. Like Nikola Tesla's relentless pursuit of innovation or Dr. Jemison's multidisciplinary approach to problem-solving, your unique perspective can lead to extraordinary outcomes when fueled by determination and creativity.

Ultimately, Limitless Horizons invite us to view life as a canvas of infinite potential, where each action contributes to a legacy of growth, transformation, and inspiration. By adopting this mindset, we not only transform our personal journey but also encourage others to break free from limitations and explore their own extraordinary paths. As we push beyond the impossible, we redefine the boundaries of human achievement and leave a lasting impact on the world. With Limitless Horizons as our guide, we step confidently into a future of boundless opportunity and infinite possibility.

"Stop arguing for your limitations"
— *Wayne Dyer*

CHAPTER 15

Embracing Infinity: Unlocking the Power of Limitless Expectations – Conclusion

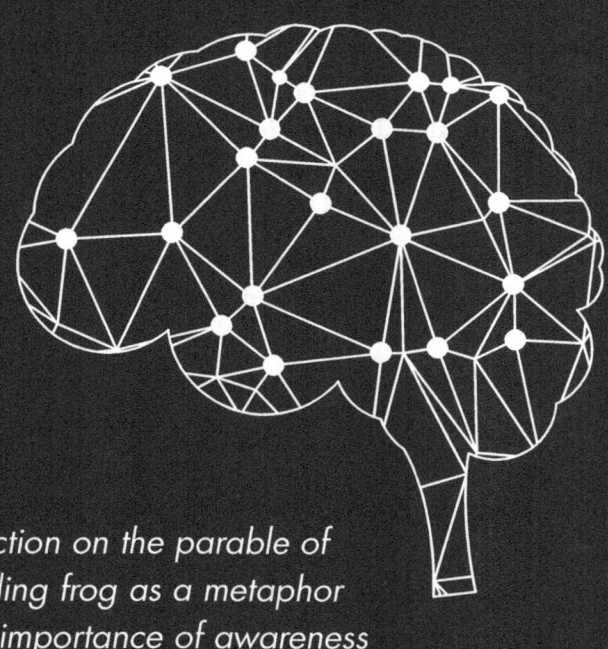

A reflection on the parable of the boiling frog as a metaphor for the importance of awareness and taking decisive action in pursuit of a boundless future.

Limitless Expectations embody the profound belief that human potential knows no bounds when we align our thoughts, actions, and beliefs with a vision of growth, success, and fulfillment. This philosophy challenges the constraints of conventional thinking, encouraging us to imagine possibilities far beyond what we once thought achievable. It's not just about dreaming big but about fostering a mindset that actively seeks opportunities in challenges, learns from failures, and continuously evolves. By adopting Limitless Expectations, we grant ourselves permission to transcend self-imposed limitations, empowering us to unlock new levels of creativity, resilience, and accomplishment.

At its core, **Limitless Expectations** align seamlessly with a growth mindset—the understanding that abilities and intelligence are not fixed traits but can be developed through effort, learning, and persistence. This perspective shifts our focus from fearing failure to embracing it as a natural and valuable part of the learning process. When coupled with purposeful action, **Limitless Expectations** enable us to tackle obstacles with confidence and curiosity, seeing them as stepping stones rather than barriers. Balancing self-compassion with accountability ensures that this journey remains sustainable, allowing us to treat ourselves with kindness while holding ourselves to the high standards necessary for meaningful growth.

The power of **Limitless Expectations** extends beyond individual transformation; it inspires a ripple effect that impacts those around us. By embracing this philosophy, we model the courage to dream boldly, the resilience to persevere, and the humility to learn from every experience. This can uplift communities and create cultures of innovation and collaboration. For example, innovators like Albert Einstein redefined what was possible by challenging conventional beliefs and pursuing breakthroughs with curiosity and determination. Through Limitless Expectations, we not only reimagine our own potential but also inspire others to do the same, contributing to a collective movement of progress, empowerment, and limitless possibilities.

Here's how **Limitless Expectations** apply to these ideas:

1. Redefining Boundaries of Belief

- **Application**: Limitless expectations begin with challenging and reshaping limiting beliefs that constrain our vision for what's possible. When we remove self-imposed ceilings, we start to imagine opportunities beyond what we previously thought achievable.
- **Relevance**: As we've discussed, tools like **Neuro-Linguistic Programming (NLP)** and visualization help rewire the mind for success. By replacing "I can't" with "I can learn how," we align with the principle that our abilities are not fixed but expandable.
- **Example**: Consider **Sammy Lee**, who shattered societal barriers and achieved greatness through innovative problem-solving. He held **limitless expectations** for himself despite external limitations, proving that mindset is often the first step toward overcoming challenges.

2. Transforming Challenges into Growth

- **Application**: **Limitless expectations** involve seeing challenges as essential catalysts for growth. This perspective aligns with **post-traumatic growth (PTG)**, where adversity fosters resilience, strength, and new perspectives.
- **Relevance**: When we approach setbacks not as barriers but as growth opportunities, we align our actions with limitless expectations. This mindset transforms fear of failure into curiosity and effort.
- **Example**: The **Apollo 13 mission** exemplifies this. Faced with catastrophic technical failures, NASA's team didn't give up—they adapted and innovated. Their **limitless expectations** of human ingenuity turned a near-disaster into a historic triumph.

3. Balancing Ambition with Compassion

- **Application**: **Limitless expectations** don't mean striving relentlessly without regard for well-being. Instead, they encourage balancing **accountability (yang)** with **self-compassion (yin)** to sustain long-term growth and fulfillment.
- **Relevance**: This balance ensures that while we hold ourselves to high standards, we also provide the emotional safety to learn from mistakes. By doing so, we prevent burnout and foster resilience.
- **Example**: **Tiger Woods** embodied this balance. After personal and professional setbacks, he used self-compassion to process his failures and accountability to rebuild his career, culminating in a historic comeback at the 2019 Masters.

4. Creating a Vision Beyond Limits

- **Application**: **Limitless expectations** fuel the creation of a vision that excites and drives us. They encourage imagining a future where success is not confined by current circumstances but guided by possibilities.
- **Relevance**: Crafting such a vision requires self-awareness, a growth mindset, and actionable steps. This echoes our discussions on visualizing success, setting boundaries, and turning setbacks into stepping stones.
- **Example**: **George Washington Carver** turned the limitations of his environment into a vision of agricultural innovation that transformed lives. His **limitless expectations** of what science and education could achieve became a legacy of empowerment.

The Core Message

Limitless Expectations apply to all facets of personal growth, inspiring us to embrace challenges, reframe failures, and align with purpose. They remind us that success isn't a static destination but a dynamic journey, fueled by curiosity, resilience, and belief in boundless potential.

Key Takeaways

1. **Challenge Limiting Beliefs**: Use tools like NLP and visualization to expand your view of what's possible.
2. **Embrace Challenges**: View struggles as opportunities for growth and transformation.
3. **Balance Compassion and Accountability**: Sustain progress without compromising mental and emotional well-being.
4. **Dream Big, Act Bigger**: Create a vision that reflects your highest aspirations and take bold steps to achieve it.

With **limitless expectations**, every obstacle becomes an opportunity, and every failure a step towards greatness. The journey starts by daring to imagine more and taking the first step toward that vision.

A Reminder to Take Action:

The parable of the **boiling frog** serves as a cautionary tale about the dangers of complacency and failing to recognize gradual, incremental changes that can lead to harm. A frog placed in a pot of water that is gradually heated to boiling will fail to notice the danger until it's too late, whereas a frog placed in boiling water immediately jumps out. This story underscores the importance of awareness, adaptability, and proactive action in the face of changing circumstances.

Key Principles and Lessons Related to the Frog Story

1. Recognizing Limiting Beliefs

Just as the frog doesn't immediately perceive the danger of the rising temperature, people can remain trapped in limiting beliefs without realizing the harm they cause. Gradually, these beliefs can erode self-confidence and prevent growth. By cultivating self-awareness and questioning our assumptions, we can identify when our mindset needs a shift.

Takeaway: Be vigilant about your thoughts and beliefs. If you notice patterns that hold you back, take proactive steps to reframe them into empowering ones.

2. Embracing Growth and Adaptability

The frog's fate results from its inability to adapt to gradual change. Similarly, individuals with a fixed mindset may struggle to adjust to new challenges or opportunities. Embracing a growth mindset allows you to see change as a stepping stone rather than a threat.

Takeaway: Commit to lifelong learning and flexibility. Growth comes from recognizing the need to change and taking consistent, intentional action.

3. Balancing Self-Compassion with Accountability

The frog's inaction mirrors how people can remain stuck in discomfort because they don't hold themselves accountable for making necessary changes. While self-compassion is essential for avoiding burnout, accountability ensures you take steps toward meaningful progress.

Takeaway: Balance kindness to yourself with the discipline to act. When you notice negative patterns or stagnation, use this awareness to make improvements.

4. The Importance of Setting Boundaries

In the story, the frog fails to recognize the point where the situation becomes harmful. Similarly, failing to set boundaries can lead to gradual burnout or unhappiness. Healthy boundaries protect your energy and well-being, enabling growth without compromise.

Takeaway: Regularly assess your environment and relationships. Are they supporting your growth, or are they slowly draining you? Adjust boundaries as needed.

5. Proactive Problem-Solving

The frog waits too long to act, missing the opportunity to save itself. This illustrates the cost of delaying action in the face of adversity. Proactive problem-solving, as seen in examples like NASA's Apollo 13 mission, highlights the value of addressing challenges head-on and adapting swiftly to avoid escalation.

Takeaway: Don't wait for circumstances to force you into action. Recognize potential issues early and address them with creativity and resolve.

Final Reflection and Takeaways

The boiling frog story reminds us that awareness and action are crucial for navigating life's challenges. By cultivating self-awareness, embracing growth, balancing compassion with accountability, and taking proactive steps, we avoid the risk of being "boiled" by gradual changes or unnoticed limitations.

- **Be Vigilant:** Regularly assess your beliefs, environment, and behaviors.
- **Stay Adaptable:** Embrace change as an opportunity to grow.
- **Act Early:** Don't wait until the "water is boiling" to make a change.
- **Set Boundaries:** Protect your energy and focus.
- **Take Ownership:** Balance self-compassion with a commitment to act.

Ultimately, the parable teaches us to leap when necessary—to recognize opportunities and challenges before they escalate. Through self-awareness and decisive action, we can escape the "pot" and pursue our potential with clarity and purpose.

Ask yourself the question, "Hey Frog how's the water?"

Here's a clever and thought-provoking way to phrase the idea! The question, "Hey Frog, how's the water?" acts as a metaphorical check-in, encouraging self-awareness and reflection on your current situation. It prompts you to assess whether you're in an environment, mindset, or circumstance that's gradually becoming harmful or stagnant, and whether you need to take action to improve or escape it.

Why It Works:

1. **Encourages Self-Awareness**
   It's a playful yet meaningful reminder to pause and evaluate. Are you comfortable, or are things subtly becoming worse without your realization?

2. **Prompts Accountability**
   By asking the question, you take ownership of recognizing the state of your "water"—your environment, thoughts, or habits.

3. **Initiates Change**
   If the answer reveals discomfort or decline, it nudges you to leap into action before the situation worsens.

Takeaway:

Regularly asking, "Hey Frog, how's the water?" keeps you mindful of gradual changes that might otherwise go unnoticed. It's a lighthearted way to remind yourself to stay aware, adaptable, and proactive in maintaining a positive and growth-oriented life.

A final Frog Metaphor:
The tragedy of the boiling frog is not the heat but its refusal to leap when the water was still warm.
— Adapted from the boiling frog parable.

Conclusion: Embracing Limitless Expectations and the Wisdom of Awareness

Limitless Expectations inspire us to recognize our boundless potential and embrace life's challenges as our personal Mount Everest—opportunities for profound growth and transformation. This philosophy teaches that our capabilities are not constrained by past failures or external circumstances but are only limited by the barriers we impose upon ourselves. By cultivating a growth mindset, aligning our actions with our values, and balancing self-compassion with accountability, we unlock the ability to transcend perceived boundaries and live authentically and purposefully.

The parable of the boiling frog is a poignant reminder of the importance of self-awareness and proactive action in pursuing limitless living. It underscores how gradual changes—be they external challenges, internal doubts, or unchecked habits—can lead to stagnation or harm if left unaddressed. The metaphor encourages us to remain vigilant, regularly assess our circumstances, and leap toward growth when necessary. "Hey Frog, how's the water?" becomes a reflective question, urging us to evaluate whether our current situation fosters growth or quietly limits our potential.

From the resilience of Albert Einstein overcoming learning challenges to the innovation of the Apollo 13 mission, the principle of limitless living is evident in history's most inspiring stories. These examples show that extraordinary achievements often stem from embracing discomfort, adapting to change, and daring to dream beyond constraints. Whether it's setting healthy boundaries, challenging limiting beliefs, or seeking continuous improvement, the path to limitless living requires intentional effort and the courage to act decisively.

The energy of gratitude also plays a vital role in this journey, as it allows us to focus on the abundance and opportunities in our lives, reinforcing a sense of fulfillment and possibility. By appreciating the gifts of the natural world, relationships, and even the lessons embedded in challenges, we cultivate a mindset of optimism and resilience. Gratitude, like limitless expectations, encourages us to see potential where others see obstacles and to act with purpose and confidence.

Key Takeaways

1. **Stay Self-Aware:** Regularly assess your mindset, environment, and actions to ensure they align with your growth and values. Ask, "Hey Frog, how's the water?"
2. **Embrace Growth:** View challenges as opportunities to refine your skills and discover new strengths.
3. **Take Decisive Action:** Don't wait for circumstances to force change—leap toward growth when you sense stagnation or harm.
4. **Cultivate Gratitude:** Focus on the abundance and opportunities in your life to reinforce positivity and resilience.
5. **Live Intentionally:** Align your actions with your highest aspirations and values to create a life of purpose and fulfillment.

The tragedy of the boiling frog is not the rising heat but its hesitation to leap when escape was still possible. **Let this serve as a reminder to recognize when your "water" no longer serves you and to act boldly in pursuit of your potential.** In doing so, you honor the philosophy **of limitless expectations**, creating a life that transcends boundaries and inspires others to believe in their own infinite possibilities.

Summary of the Book and Final Chapter

This book is an exploration of the transformative concept of **Limitless Expectations**, emphasizing that the reality we experience is deeply influenced by the beliefs we hold and the actions we take. Each chapter offers practical tools and inspiring examples to help readers break free from self-imposed limitations, embrace challenges as opportunities, and reprogram their minds for success. By cultivating a growth mindset, balancing self-compassion with accountability, and aligning actions with purpose, readers are guided to unlock their boundless potential and redefine what is possible.

From the Wright brothers' revolutionary flight to leaders like Nikola Tesla who dared to reimagine the limits of science and innovation, this book demonstrates that history's most profound achievements stem from visionary thinking and bold action. It explores the interconnected roles of Emotional and Spiritual Intelligence in navigating relationships and challenges, as well as the power of gratitude and self-awareness to shift perspectives and foster resilience. Together, these principles form a roadmap for personal transformation, inviting readers to expand their vision beyond the impossible and take meaningful steps toward living a limitless life.

Final Words: Embracing Infinity

In the final chapter, **Embracing Infinity: Unlocking the Power of Limitless Expectations**, the essence of this philosophy is distilled into a powerful call to action. The parable of the boiling frog serves as a metaphor for the dangers of complacency and the importance of self-awareness. Just as the frog's inability to act leads to its downfall, so too can unnoticed patterns, unchecked habits, or ignored challenges quietly limit our growth. Asking yourself, "Hey Frog, how's the water?" is a simple yet profound practice of reflection that encourages you to remain vigilant and make changes when necessary.

Limitless Expectations reminds us that our only true limits are the realities we choose to manifest. By reprogramming our minds to focus on opportunities rather than obstacles, we create a foundation for growth and innovation. As the stories of visionaries throughout history demonstrate, greatness is achieved not by avoiding challenges but by facing them with boldness, resilience, and the belief that failure is simply a step toward success.

To cultivate this mindset, embrace self-awareness, gratitude, and intentionality in all that you do. Be willing to challenge limiting beliefs, take risks, and surround yourself with people who inspire you to think bigger and act bolder. Remember that every leap toward growth, no matter how small, contributes to the larger vision of a life filled with purpose, fulfillment, and limitless horizons.

Ultimately, the journey to limitless living is one of courage, imagination, and persistence. Whether you are launching a bold new project, seeking deeper connections, or confronting adversity, know that the power to transcend limitations lies within you. **Your only limits are the realities you choose to manifest.** Let this truth inspire you to leap into the unknown, reimagine what is possible, and create a legacy that transforms both your life and the world around you.

"The only limits to our realization of tomorrow will be our doubts of today. Let us move forward with strong and active faith."
— *Franklin D. Roosevelt*

www.ingramcontent.com/pod-product-compliance
Lightning Source LLC
Chambersburg PA
CBHW060340170426
43202CB00014B/2833